D0486435

Never Wipe Your Ass with a Squirrel

A Trail Running, Ultramarathon, and Wilderness

Survival Guide for Weird Folks

By Jason Robillard

Never Wipe Your Ass with a Squirrel:
A trail running, ultramarathon, and wilderness survival guide for weird folks

First edition

© 2013, Jason Robillard
Barefoot Running Press
(robillardj@gmail.com)

About My Editors

This project would not be possible if not for the generous contributions from my talented editing team. I used a slightly different editing model for the Squirrel Wipe project. Instead of using a single editor or series of editors, I solicited the services of several editors at the same time, then chose which edits to add from each. The goal was to maintain the "came from a blog" feel without watering down the final product. Here are my editors:

- **Jeff Fite-** Jeff is a research psychologist for the U.S. Army, and routinely edits for academic journals.
- **Vanessa Rodriguez-** Vanessa is a fellow ultrarunner and provided valuable running-specific feedback. Check out Vanessa's excellent book *The Summit Seeker* describing her journey that eventually led to a nomadic ultrarunning lifestyle much like Shelly and I have done. Check out Vanessa's blog: http://vanessaruns.com.
- **Trisha Reeves-** Trisha's editing may have finally broken my tendency to use "that" when referring to people! Check out Trisha's blog: http://barefoot-monologues.com/
- **Anna Toombs-** Anna provided valuable "Across the Pond" editing from the UK. Check out Anna's barefoot running site: http://www.barefootrunninguk.com/.
- **Ressie Stranley-** Ressie is a friend from my younger years and provided excellent editing tips.

Other Acknowledgments

I never would have attempted a project like this if it were not for Shelly's unwavering support and occasional tough love. My life is one awesome adventure after another, and I have her to thank.

Many of the pictures from the book were taken or edited by Stephanie Smedberg. Also, Shelly and I couldn't have done many of our adventures without her assistance.

I also have to thank my ultrarunning friends... even those that don't really run much. Jesse Scott, Jeremiah Cataldo, Christian and Amy Peterson, Jon Sanregret, Shacky, Vanessa, Mark Robillard, Phil Stapert, Tim Looney, Nate Wolfe, Brandon Mulnix, Krista Cavendar, John DeVries, Stuart Peterson, Pete Larson, Mark Cucuzzella, Tony Schaub, Chip Tilden, Pat Sweeney, Bill Katovsky, Damian Stoy, James Barstad, Mark Lofquist, Gordy Ainsleigh, Emily Snayd, Dave Repp, Ken Bob Saxton, Rick Robbins, Tucker Goodrich, TJ Gerken, Michael Helton, Josh Sutcliffe, William Garabrant, Ted MacDonald, Heather Wiatrowski, Shelley Viggiano, Kate Kift, Bob Nicol, Buzz and Sarah Johnson, Chase Williams, and all the rest of the ultrarunners I've had the pleasure of sharing the trails with over the years. You folks taught me everything I know.

Table of Contents

Introduction

Trail running has been a major passion of mine for years. It has been such an obsession, my wife Shelly and I quit our jobs as high school teachers to chase the adventure of discovering new trails, climbing mountains, drinking water from questionable sources, and thoroughly exploring the many wonderful RV parks spread across the United States. That journey proved to be a life-changing experience. It affirmed our love of the trails, streams, mountains, and other natural phenomena that blanket the landscape. It also taught us many lessons about life in general and trail running in particular.

I'm a teacher at heart. I couldn't experience all that I've experienced without sharing with the world. My goal is simple- I want to get people outside. I want people to escape the concrete jungle. I want people to experience the natural wonder that surrounds us. I want people to explore the forests, canyons, and mountains. I want people to reconnect with nature. And I want them to have fun in the process. This book is one of my tools to help make that goal a reality. It started as a series of blog posts on my Squirrel Wipe and Barefoot Running University websites, and has been expanded to the current format.

This book will provide a basic introduction to the various elements of trail and ultramarathon running. It's not an exhaustive collection of every bit of knowledge that exists. You can find that shit on the Internet. It's also not a personal account of my own experiences. If you want that, find Shelly and I and buy us a beer or two. I *do* draw on my own experiences repeatedly, but only to document my experimentation successes and failures. The book will provide fodder for your own experimentation. It's not about me. *It's about you.*

I'm not an elite ultrarunner. On the best of days, I barely crack "mediocre." I'm just an average dude doing things that may *seem* extraordinary... but they're not. Trail running and ultras are something almost anyone can do if they mix the right ingredients. I managed to find my own right mix despite having a full-time job, three kids, a semi-pro writing writing and blogging gig, and a somewhat lazy disposition.

This book is a tool that will give *you* a foundation that will allow you to build your own experiences that fit your particular life situation. Unlike most ultra books, I largely ignore conventional wisdom in favor of my own special brand of dumbassery. Most other trail and ultra books are written by really good ultrarunners that either have a biological advantage, a lot more free time, or just flat out work harder than the rest of us. The advice is great, but never quite works as well as advertised. Other trail and ultra books are nothing more than elaborate race reports where runners discuss their own personal journey. They glorify their running experiences to the point where you'd think they were writing about curing cancer or bringing peace to the Middle East. This is, after all, just a hobby. Both formats can be useful and are fascinating, but aren't always the best teaching tools.

When reading the book, imagine you're part of a small group of people sitting around a high-top table in the corner of a dive bar pounding pitcher after pitcher of some local IPA while discussing the gory details of trail and ultrarunning. I'm like the drunk dude that's twenty pounds overweight, thinks he's funnier than he really is, and is willing to do anything if dared. I ignore social mores, tact, and any feelings of shame. I tackle shit (literally in some cases) other ultrarunning writers largely ignore. Some may help. Some will hurt. All will help you learn.

Many of these topics are a direct result of my own experiences with experimentation, and I like to explain them in graphic detail using occasional crude language. Remember the bar scenario? Keep that visual in mind as you read. If you have a Tucker Max book on your coffee table, find Sarah Silverman hilarious, enjoy being naked, or have ever woken up face-down on your neighbor's front lawn, you'll appreciate the book.

If you don't like to laugh, wear a monocle and describe yourself as "stoic", spend lots of free time at Bible study, enjoy jigsaw puzzles of Mongolian landscapes, list "Full House" as your all-time favorite TV show, and don't have the ability to laugh at yourself, you'll probably be disappointed. And repeatedly offended.

Embrace the format. It's up to you to learn as much as you can, then figure out what works for you. Experiment. Keep the stuff that works. Eliminate the stuff that doesn't. Figure out what works for *YOU*. Trail running is a journey, not a destination. *Savor the learning experience.*

Oh, and the book title? I have my friend Pablo Päster to thank for that. It stemmed from a discussion about the lack of wiping materials in the back country. Squirrels are a poor choice mostly due to their "grabby" hands. I was going to change the book title to something more appropriate, but my twisted friends convinced me otherwise. I love you guys!

Enjoy!

-Jason

Why DO People Run Trails?

Most runners don't seem to gravitate toward trails until they've already gained some experience as a runner. The reasons for exploring trail running are as varied as the individuals who take the plunge into the wilderness. Here are a few:

- **Runners want to reconnect with nature.** Our hurried, frantic lives are filled with noise, clutter, and busy schedules. The quiet solitude of nature provides a welcome reprieve from the daily grind.
- **The trails are easier on your body.** Road running requires monotonous movements repeated time and time again over an unforgiving, unchanging surface. Trail running, with endless variety, often-times softer surfaces, and more dynamic movements gives the body a welcomed break.
- **Obstacle courses and mud runs no longer offer enough challenge.** While these man-made runs offer interesting challenges, climbing over walls, negotiating balance beams, and crawling through mud only provides a finite replay value. Trail running offers an ever-changing obstacle course crafted by Mother Nature.
- **Adventure.** Trail running can be quite dangerous depending on location. The possibility of great bodily harm or even death can be exhilarating.
- **Glory.** Okay, there's not too much glory in the trail running world. But there is camaraderie.
- **Camaraderie.** By virtue of venturing into dangerous locations, trail runners tend to live by a code. We look out for each other. This results in a sense of fellowship that's difficult to find in other variations of running.

Shelly, Gordy, Shacky, and Vanessa at Loch Leven Lakes, CA

What is a Trail?

A trail can be defined in a variety of ways. I prefer a simple diagnostic method called the "Christian Peterson test"- can you easily push a baby stroller over the trail?

If so, it's *not* a trail. If not, it's a trail.

This definition rules out paved bike paths, crushed limestone trails, and wooden boardwalks. It's not a perfect operational definition, but it serves the purpose. The distinction is necessary because the non-trails share more in common with road running. But if you regularly run on non-trail surfaces, many of the topics covered in this book will still be helpful.

Technical Trails versus Non-technical Trails

The term "technical" is used to describe the relative "roughness" or difficulty of a particular trail. Unfortunately, no standard measure exists. When I lived in the Midwest, we called our most difficult trails "technical." However, trail runners in the rugged mountains of Eastern Tennessee would likely consider the Midwest trails to be non-technical. To help clear up this confusion, I like to use the following definitions:

- **Non-technical**: This includes any trail that is free of obstacles or debris. It would be possible to sprint down this trail without worry of tripping. The ultramarathon community sometimes refers to these trails as "runnable."
- **Moderately technical**: Moderately technical trails have some debris that may require a runner to alter their gait. Rocks and roots are the most common debris. Most of a moderately technical trail is runnable, though occasional walking may be required.
- **Technical**: Technical trails are covered with considerable debris. Running at full speed may be nearly impossible, but some running is possible. Technical trails may include occasional climbs that require the use of hands.
- **Extremely technical**: Extremely technical trails are not runnable most of the time. The debris is frequent and dangerous. The trail may require significant climbing with the aid of hands.

How Does Trail Running Compare to Other Activities?

Trail running is similar to road running or obstacle course racing, only more challenging. It also shares the "getting back to nature" aspect of some activities like hiking, camping, or rock climbing.

Trail running is more dynamic than road running. Road running usually involves repeating the same motion again and again for a period of time. You deal with cars, people, and other potentially unsavory aspects of civilization. Trail running adds the element of dynamic movements needed to run up and down hills, through mud and water, and over rocks, roots, and other obstacles.

Trail running is also more dynamic and unpredictable than obstacle course running. Many people transition to obstacle course running because road running becomes too boring, and they needed a new challenge. Others turn to obstacle course running because they enjoy functional fitness type activities (e.g. Crossfit.) These races provide a cardiovascular AND strength component, which is missing in each individual activity. Trail running provides MORE of the experience. Think of trail running as a graduate course in obstacle course running.

Finally, trail running provides the serene nature experience of hiking, camping, and rock climbing without the need for a ton of gear. That lack of gear generally allows for more ground to be covered in a shorter period of time.

Trail Etiquette

Lots of road runners seem to be making the jump to trail running. This is a great thing! Unfortunately many of these runners carry some bad road running habits over to the trails. I'll cover this topic in great detail throughout the rest of the book, but here's a quick and dirty (pun intended) guide for new trail runners that are impatient:

1. Don't be afraid of dirt. I've watched runners in squeaky-white sneakers tiptoe around a tiny mud puddle. I've seen new trail runners on the verge of vomiting when watching a veteran trail runner bomb through knee-deep mud. These are trails. We get dirty. It's a badge of honor. Wear it with pride.

2. Don't litter. Ever. Don't toss that Gu packet on the ground. Throw your cup in the aid station waste basket. Don't blow your nose and throw the tissue on the trail. Someone has to pick up after you, and it's douchey to expect volunteers to clean up after your mess. It may be acceptable to toss your shit anywhere on the roads, but we live by a different code out here. Respect the environment.

3. If someone needs help, help them. If another runner is in obvious pain, lost, crying, or otherwise in distress, stop and help. I've watched the leaders of trail races stop to help others, even if they lose their position as a result. We take care of each other. It's the decent human thing to do.

4. If taking a leak or dropping a deuce, get off the trail. This one needs no explanation.

5. Be courteous when passing or getting passed. When passing another runner on a single track (narrow trail), the passing runner should say something along the lines of "passing on the left", then pass OFF THE TRAIL. The runner being passed, when hearing this, may step off to the right and allow the faster runner to pass. Only then is it acceptable for the passing runner to remain on the trail. If a runner approaches another from behind, it's courteous to acknowledge their presence and ask him or her if they'd like to pass. Also, always remember- those going faster always yield to those going slower. That means all runners yield to horses.

6. Thank volunteers. They're giving their time to YOU. Be grateful. Say thanks. Give them a high-five. Joke around with them. Make them feel appreciated.

7. Don't expect to be treated like a prima donna. You're one of many runners running that particular race. Making unreasonable demands or expecting people to cater to your crazy-ass needs isn't your divine right. In fact, it makes you look like an ass. And it ruins the day for those of us that want to have a good time.

8. Be humble. No matter what you do, someone has gone longer or done it faster. It's okay to be proud of your accomplishments, but don't talk about them incessantly. Instead of starting a conversation by bragging about your accomplishments, ask others about theirs. You might learn something. The only time it's acceptable to bring up your accomplishments is to put a bragging douche in their place. Even then, use it sparingly.

9. Smile. If you're frowning, grimacing, or expressing any other negative emotion (aside from pain if it's a long race), you're doing it wrong. Cheer up little buckaroo... you're surrounded by awesome people and breathtaking nature. Trail running is about camaraderie and mutual support. It's about being a small part of something bigger than yourself. That's what makes it special. You can make your contribution by kicking back, taking it easy, and going with the flow.

Trail Runner Jon Sanregret

Trailcraft

Trailcraft is the art of navigating a trail using a variety of skills. The goal is to run trails effectively and efficiently without wasting a ton of energy, tripping, or falling off a cliff. Road runners have the luxury of largely ignoring their path. The road is predictable. If they zone out or stare off into space, there's little danger.

Trail running is different. It requires diligent focus on the path ahead. There are obstacles that present real danger. Rocks, roots, branches, streams, cliffs, small woodland creatures... all present a possible threat. The key to successfully running trails comes down to one idea:

10

Pay attention to your foot placement!

Ideally, we'd always like to be able to see where we will place our foot with each step. There are three variables that control this: vision, ground feel, and the density of obstacles on the trail.

The ability to see where you're running is important, but not always necessary. With experience, it's possible to run in complete darkness by relying on the ability to feel the ground with each step. This ability decreases with speed and difficulty of terrain. On very technical trails, like the type with sharp rocks, vision is critical. Not only do you have to see where each foot will land, you also have to assure the other foot has a place to land. You have to "see" two steps ahead. If you're wrong about step one and inadvertently step on a sharp rock, you can mitigate the damage by relaxing and taking the pressure off that foot. That requires the other foot to land to maintain balance, which is why you have to assure that foot has a place to land. If vision is obscured to the point where you cannot "see" that second step, running becomes almost impossible. This may be due to darkness, snow covering hard ice, leaves covering rocks, etc.

Sidebar #1- Some people have asked why I use a handheld flashlight when trail running at night. It allows me to discriminate terrain better than a headlamp. With headlamps, the light source is close to my eyes. It's nearly impossible to see shadows and depth, which makes the terrain appear flat (2D.) With the light source away from my eyes, the depth of shadows allows me to determine the height and shape of obstacles (3D.) Also, the ability to quickly move the light up and down and side to side can eliminate ambiguity.

Sidebar #2- Some people also ask why I spread my arms when running downhill. The quick answer: Balance. The longer answer: maintaining balance if I happen to step on something sharp with that first step. If I'm running fast downhill and step on something sharp, the "relax" reflex kicks in and my other foot immediately searches for a landing spot to maintain balance. Since I'm going fast, I'm outrunning my ability to "see" where the second foot lands. If *that* foot lands on something sharp, I'm falling. The outstretched arms help me balance which keeps that fall in the "stumble" category as opposed to the "I'm losing teeth when my head bounces off the ground" category.

Vision is also influenced by sleep deprivation and fatigue. Your tired brain's ability to interpret incoming sensory signals decreases as a function of fatigue and sleep deprivation. These are two factors that make 100 milers so difficult.

When vision is reduced or eliminated completely, the ability to navigate technical terrain decreases. At some point, trail running with limited vision becomes almost impossible.

Ground feel is *almost* as important as vision. This is the ability to immediately and correctly identify what is under foot. In many cases, this is an unconscious, reflexive action. The millisecond you step on something, your feet identify it as something that causes pain or doesn't cause pain and whether the surface is flat, cambered, or the footing is otherwise compromised. If the surface isn't even, your body reacts by preventing further downward force. If it is pretty good, your body continues loading the foot as your weight shifts over that leg. Also, if landing on an uneven surface, you will know by both the tactile sensation (part of the foot is touching a surface, part is not) and a proprioceptive sensation (foot is inverting, ankle is flexing, etc.) These bodily sensations prevent sprained ankles and allow you to run quickly over uneven surfaces.

"Feel" is always a tradeoff of wearing shoes versus being barefoot (which IS possible.) The protection provided by shoes allows you a larger margin of error with foot placement. However, any protection you gain is met with a corresponding loss of tactile and proprioceptive sensation, which often affects the running form in trail runners. The thicker the shoe, the less ground feel you get. This is the reason shoe selection becomes a tricky proposition- you have to weigh the costs and benefits of an increase in protection versus a decrease in ground feel.

"Feel" is also influenced by sleep deprivation and fatigue for the same reason as vision. If you have adequate vision, you can run without any ground feel at all.

The density of the obstacles is more important than the characteristics of the obstacles themselves. I'll use the example of sharp gravel covering an asphalt road. If the gravel is so dense you step on many pieces with each step, running is easy. You get a "bed of nails" effect where many pointy surfaces are contacting your foot. The cumulative surface area distributes your weight enough to prevent pain or injury. This is why it's relatively easy to learn to run on asphalt.

Running becomes more difficult when the gravel density is thin enough where you always step on a few pieces but thick enough to make it impossible to avoid. The same concept holds true for overly technical trails. Small, sharp rocks usually aren't a problem. Neither are huge rocks. It's the golf ball to softball size sharp rocks that usually cause the problems.

Elements of Good Running Form

Good running form is one of the most neglected elements of running. For decades, we've followed a paradigm where we use various shoe designs to correct bad running form. The rise of barefoot and minimalist shoe running has created a surge of research that has progressively shifted the paradigm. We're now moving toward the idea of learning good form, then selecting shoes that don't interfere with good form. It's a subtle but significant difference.

So what is "good form?" This is a tricky issue. What works for some may not work for others. Most seem to agree on some points, however. Here are the basics that most people agree are the foundation for better running form:

1. Upright posture. Good posture is the foundation of good form. Your posture should be upright, your arms should swing freely at your sides, and your knees should remain bent throughout the gait cycle.
2. Feet landing under your body. It's common for people to overstride where their foot lands in front of their body. This is less efficient and dramatically increases the impact of running. It also reduces balance, which is critically important when trail running.
3. Faster, shorter steps. Your cadence, or number of steps per minute, should increase to at least 180 per minute. Your stride length should also decrease. This helps insure your feet will land under your body.

Making these adjustments will increase your efficiency and likely reduce injuries regardless of the shoes you have on your feet. While I'm a huge proponent of running barefoot and in minimalist "barefoot" shoes, they may not be appropriate for everyone. Even if you wear motion-control cushioned trainers with a huge raised heel, making these changes to your running form can make a dramatic difference.

Want to learn the nitty-gritty details? Check out my other wildly popular book *The Barefoot Running Book* (Plume, 2012.)

Run Efficiently

Learning good form will definitely help you to become more efficient. This will allow you to run faster and longer by expending less energy. This idea can be taken further by thinking of ultrarunning as an exercise in efficiency. Your goal should be to expend as little energy as possible.

When I race, I try to eliminate as many wasted movements as I can. I only lift my feet high enough to clear the highest obstacle on the trail. When running up and down hills, I try to relax my muscles as much as possible and take short, easy steps. I limit my arm swing to the absolute minimum. Every wasted movement burns more precious calories.

You can incorporate efficiency by actively focusing on running as smoothly as possible. Good form, as discussed earlier, will create a noticeable difference in energy expenditure. Always look for other ways to reduce movement. For example, I tie my shoes in double knots so I won't have to re-tie them during the race. It's a tiny detail, but many of those little details can add up.

Difference Between Road Running Gait and Trail Running Gait

Road running and trail running are dramatically different skills. Road running requires using the same gait for a long period of time. You're stressing a relatively small number of muscles repeatedly. Trail running requires a much more dynamic gait. Because you have to jump around the trail to avoid obstacles like rocks, roots, and water, you stress a large number of muscles in various combinations.

When road runners run trails for the first time, they're often struck by the difficulty of utilizing different muscle groups. The same phenomenon happens when trail runners run roads for the first time.

If you train in conditions you'll likely experience during a race, this will not be an issue. However, I would advise any runner to add at least one run per week on a different surface. Road runners should occasionally hit the trails. Trail runners should occasionally hit the road. It will dramatically enhance your ability to switch between the two.

For my first 50 miler, I trained almost exclusively on roads. The trails killed me. Over the last few years, I've shied away from road running. Whenever I run a road race, it takes much longer to recover.

Uphill Technique

Unless you do all your running in Florida, you will probably encounter the occasional hill. How should you approach the hill? Should you modify your technique? Does it depend on the surface? Are there other important variables? Let's find out.

The Basics

The single biggest mistake people make when running uphill is an elongated stride. People take steps that are too big. The longer the step you take, the more energy you'll expend over that distance. It's more efficient to take two shorter steps instead of one longer step. You can experiment with this idea by running up a flight of stairs. Hit each step on the first trip up. Then try taking two steps at a time. Then try three. Which condition was the easiest?

Posture

Posture shouldn't change from your flat-ground running gait. There's no need to lean forward or lean back. In fact, doing either will upset your balance and increase the likelihood of falling. Keep your back straight and your head up. Resist the urge to bend at the waist as this stresses the lower back.

Power Hiking

I power hike steep hills in training and all hills in long races. It's more efficient than running. The power hike is a bit of a misnomer, because you're not really "powering" up the hill. The movements require very little muscle activation. Take very short (3-8″) steps. When your foot is planted on the ground, use your glutes to lift your body up and forward over your planted foot. This motion can be assisted by straightening your knee. I like to visualize my knee moving backward to move from the bent to the straight position.

Most people seem to use their quads to power hike, which causes premature fatigue. It's common to hear runners complain of "trashed quads." You know you're doing it right if you can climb a hill of any length without experiencing excessive muscle soreness or fatigue.

Running

If the hill isn't especially steep or you're running a shorter distance, you can maintain a running gait when climbing. Like power hiking, posture doesn't change. I don't change other elements of gait except stride length and cadence. Like power hiking, I'll take shorter, faster steps instead of longer, slower steps. The same efficiency concept applies.

The muscle activation pattern is close to the same, too. I don't rely on my quads to "power" up the hill. Instead, I use my glutes to lift my body up and forward. It's a far more resilient muscle group.

Foot Placement

This lesson applies mostly to trails. When the trail gets too steep, your foot can't dorsiflex (pulling your foot up toward your shin) enough to keep your heel on the ground (see the first picpicture). I always look for the flattest grades to place my feet whether I'm running or power hiking. I'll use debris like sticks, roots, and rocks as "steps." The purpose is to limit the dorsiflexion of the foot (see second picture). If your foot dorsiflexes too much, it strains your calf muscles and Achilles tendon.

Heel comes off the ground because of steep grade

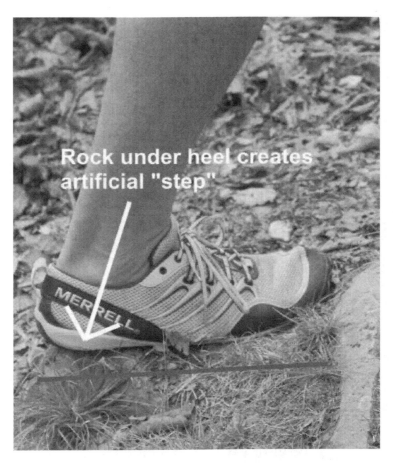

Rock under heel creates artificial "step"

I also try to get as much of my foot on the ground as possible for maximum traction. Slipping down the hill wastes energy. If your foot begins to slip, quickly place your other foot on the ground and shift the weight to that foot.

Picking Your Line

Like foot placement, picking your line is more of a trail running issue. Many runners just run or hike up hills with little regard for the "line", or route, they choose. Instead of just picking a random path, use the terrain to your advantage. I borrowed this technique from Jesse Scott. Use the same "short step" technique I discussed above and pick out a line that requires the shortest steps. In other words, avoid a line that requires you to take large steps, especially if you're stepping on or over a large rock, root, or log.

Practicing

The best way to master going uphill is to practice frequently. I spent several months training with a heart rate monitor to gauge my technique. I'd climb a hill at a specific pace and measure my average heart rate. Then I'd try a slightly different technique and measure that average heart rate. I'd compare the techniques and use the one that was most efficient. I would then test that technique on some really long mountain climbs (3 to 6 miles). If you don't live near mountains, a treadmill set on 12-15 percent grade will work. If I felt any muscle fatigue, I practiced keeping those muscles relaxed.

Using this methodology, I was able to fine-tune my technique to the point where I can climb pretty much any hill with ease. It's been a major reason I've been able to run 100 milers on relatively low training mileage.

Downhill Technique

After years of experimentation, I finally stumbled upon two good techniques to assist downhill running. First, I shift my weight backward by pulling my shoulders back a little bit... sort of like pinching my shoulder blades together. Second, I "sit back" slightly like I'm sitting in a chair. Since this subject is much more difficult to visualize than uphill technique, I demonstrate the idea in this YouTube video:

http://www.youtube.com/watch?v=oDSrUyzFPKc

On very steep terrain, I may utilize the "ski technique" discussed in the second part of the video. I basically mimic the back-and-forth twisting of a downhill skier negotiating moguls. It's slow, but effectively allows more of the foot to come in contact with the ground, which increases control. If I start sliding, it's easier to regain control.

Mud

Running through mud can be problematic for a few reasons. It may be slippery. It could clog the tread on your shoes. If it's deep enough, you could get stuck. Worse, the mud could suck your shoes off your feet. If you're running a long race, the mud can infiltrate your shoe. And, if the mud dries inside your shoe, it leaves a gritty, abrasive mess.

Despite all of these drawbacks, mud is pretty damn fun. I only avoid mud if there's a potential to disrupt my race goals. Otherwise I just bomb through it with a smile on my face.

Not all mud is the same, though. Some types of mud is worse than other types. A basic familiarity with mud properties can be very helpful. Here are some basics:

- **Know the local soil.** If an area has a lot of clay content, the mud will be exceedingly slippery and sticky. I try to avoid this mud on long runs or longish races. If you're running in an area with rich soil with lots of lush plants and trees, mud is usually thick. This mud usually isn't too bad as long as the mud holes aren't too deep. The shade from trees slows drying time, so mud holes may be rather deep. If the area has

20

sandy soil, mud is usually thin and gritty. I almost always run through this stuff.

- **Know what reflectivity indicates.** Wet mud with a *shiny appearance* is fresh. And wet. And usually deep. A *dull surface* indicates mud that is drying. This is almost always safe to run over.
- **Know what's under the mud.** Mud may be covering sharp rocks (which is why it's not a good idea to run barefoot on some muddy trails), ruts from vehicle tires, hoof prints from cattle, etc. When your foot hits the mud, your brain registers it as a flat surface and proceeds to shift all your weight on that foot. As you sink through the mud, the uneven underlying surface could cause serious injuries like ankle sprains. Worse, sharp rocks may be hidden. As the foot slips, the rocks may slice your foot to shreds. My friend Nate Wolfe ran an entire race barefoot in these conditions. The results weren't pretty.

Trail erosion can also be a concern. In some areas such as the trails surrounding Boise, Idaho, trail running on muddy trails is prohibited because it speeds erosion. In other areas like the Colorado Rockies, runners are usually encouraged to stay on muddy trails to prevent damage to the plants along the trail. In the Midwest, it's common to leave the trail to bypass mud holes. Be familiar with your area's rules and customs.

Shoe choice in muddy conditions is an important consideration. A cleated sole usually helps, but the cleats have to be far enough apart to prevent mud from caking between the knobs. Also, a shoe that drains well is useful. If water and mud enter the shoe, you want a mechanism in place to allow the mud and water to escape. Newbies sometimes experiment with waterproof shoes. In my experience, anything that keeps water out also keeps it in. Since mud and water easily flow over the top of the shoe, waterproof shoes are more or less useless.

Snow and Ice

Snow and ice introduce many of the same concerns as mud. Slipping is the greatest danger, followed by wet feet. Like mud, snow composition changes based on environmental conditions. Snow may be wet and "packy", powdery, or packed down and frozen. Each condition presents unique challenges.

- **Wet snow:** Wet snow causes everything to get wet, which usually equates to "cold." I treat this snow much like mud. It's slippery. Unless it's compressed (like on a well-used trail), it is difficult to run through due to resistance.
- **Powder:** Since the moisture content of powdery snow is low, it doesn't drench shoes and clothing. It also doesn't provide much resistance when running through deep sections. The greatest problem is vision-powdery snow obscures the underlying surface. Since the snow is so thin, the layer that's compressed under foot does little to buffer hidden objects.
- **Hard-packed snow:** There's a fine line between compressed, hard-packed snow and ice. Functionally they present the same problem-slipperiness. If the surface is flat, good running form should prevent most slips because your feet will always land under your center of gravity. If the surface isn't flat, like hills or cambered surfaces, shortening your stride can help prevent falling.

If you live in a cold climate, be careful with ice-covered surfaces. As a general rule of thumb, you should never attempt to cross ice thinner than about two inches. Since most runners don't carry ice-boring tools, a stick can be used to test ice. Try driving the stick through the ice. If it breaks through, don't cross. If the ice cracks, it's probably not strong enough to support your body weight. If it doesn't crack, it should be safe to cross.

Still water freezes faster than flowing water. As such, lakes and ponds are generally safer to cross than rivers or streams. Wind also affects freezing water. In windy conditions, the churning water won't freeze as quickly as still water.

In the event you fall through ice, don't panic. Don't remove clothing as it traps air and aids in floatation. Turn toward the direction you came from, reach your arms across the ice, and kick your legs and crawl with your arms to "swim" out of the hole. Once you get out, roll to the edge of the shore. Rolling distributes more weight than walking or crawling, which will help prevent breaking through again. Get out of the cold as soon as possible as hypothermia sets in quickly. Build a fire if needed. If clothing is damp, dry it out. Wet t-shirts may be desirable for spring break in Cancun or Lake Havasu, but they can be deadly in the frozen wilderness.

Water Crossings

Trail runners occasionally encounter water crossings. These may range from a trickle of a stream to a raging river. Knowing some properties of flowing water will help you determine if a crossing is safe and what technique should be used.

Small jumpable crossings

If the crossing is small enough, just jump over it. Make sure the footing on either bank is adequate for pushing off and landing. If there's mud, use caution. Shiny mud is slippery mud. If other runners have already jumped across, it may be best to move a few feet up or down stream.

Moderate crossings that cannot be jumped

For larger streams, you may have to hop on rocks or logs to cross, or just step in the stream. Footing is the most important consideration. It's usually best to stop, assess the options, then cross cautiously. If it is possible to hop across using rocks or logs, make sure the footing is good. Wet rocks and logs will be slippery. Smaller rocks may wobble. Old logs may be rotten. Both may be covered with algae, moss, or other such slimy substances. If possible, test each step before fully committing all of your body weight. If the footing is questionable, just step IN the stream. A wet foot is better than slipping and falling.

Crossings that require you to get wet

These crossings range from wide streams to rivers. If you encounter such a crossing, assess the safety of the crossing. The speed of the current is a major consideration. The faster the current the more dangerous the crossing. Debris like sticks, logs, and plant matter are good indicators of flow rate.

Also consider the footing in the stream or river. Mud may cause you to sink, lose a shoe, or get stuck. Sharp rocks could cause foot injuries. Flat rocks could be slippery.

Knowing the properties of streams and rivers can help determine a safe crossing point. The goal is to find the shallowest crossing. This is almost always found in straight, wide sections. The deepest areas of flowing bodies of water are found on the *outer* edge of bends. Anything more than knee-deep can easily sweep you off your feet. Also consider the entry and exit points. Make sure you will be able to safely enter and exit the water.

When crossing, face toward the current. Maintain balance by shuffling your feet. Using a stick as a pole will help maintain balance. If you get swept off your feet, keep your head facing upstream and swim toward the closest shore.

If you're part of a group and the crossing is especially dangerous, you can utilize the "linked-arm" technique. By linking arms and using the technique described above, you can help each other maintain balance as you cross. Imagine the "We are the World" folks. Now imagine we throw them into a wild river.

A note about parasites

In some delicate ecosystems, crossing multiple streams should be avoided due to invasive species transmission. Crossing one stream will pick up some tiny travelers which can then be deposited in another stream. This probably isn't a concern unless you're running very long distances. If you ARE crossing multiple streams and there's a concern with cross-contamination, change your shoes between crossings or use a disinfecting agent. In my experience, this is only a concern in high mountain zones where people seem to care about the preservation of the local ecology. In many areas, we just rely on toxic waste run-off from factories to kill invasive species.

Altitude

Some of the world's best trails are found in mountains. The spectacular scenery, deep blue skies, and solitude are nothing short of amazing. Unfortunately mountain running has a serious drawback- thin air. The higher the altitude, the lower the oxygen content of the air we breathe. The thinner the air, the more problems humans develop.

Altitude sickness has a few common symptoms including breathlessness, nausea, dizziness, headaches, loss of appetite, trouble sleeping, and muscle weakness. It IS possible to die from altitude sickness (via pulmonary or cerebral edema.)

Altitude sickness is not necessarily universal; it only affects a certain percentage of the population. There are no reliable predictors to determine susceptibility other than a lack of acclimation. People who live at or near sea level and then venture to high altitudes experience the problems.

Symptoms typically begin around 5,000 to 6,000 feet up to about 8,000 feet. The higher the altitude, the more severe the symptoms.

Prevention

The best way to prevent altitude sickness is acclimation, which involves spending time at altitude. Spending several weeks at the desired altitude will usually prevent most problems. Slowly increasing the ascent can also help. For example, if you're racing at 12,000 feet, spend a few days at 6,000 feet, then 8,000, then 10,000 feet. If that's not possible, running within 24 hours of arrival at altitude is usually desirable.

Staying well-hydrated can also prevent altitude sickness symptoms. Drink lots of water and avoid diuretics like caffeine and alcohol.

Some drugs such as acetazolamide, dexamethasone, sumatriptan, and Myo-inositol trispyrophosphate (ITPP) may help treat or even prevent symptoms. However, like most drugs, they may have undesirable side effects that could inhibit athletic performance. There are products that supposedly ease acclimation problems, but I'd recommend a skeptical approach. Self-experimentation with and without supplements should be enough to assess the validity of any marketing claims.

Pooping

"What happens when I have to... you know, take a #2?"

Shelly and Krista Cavender watching Pablo Paster demonstrating a decent poop squat

I am a little surprised this question does not come up more often. Here's the situation- you're thirty miles into a 50 mile run. You're surrounded by nothing but untamed wilderness. You have to drop a deuce. Since there are no porta-potties for another 20 miles, you are left with no choice but to drop drawers and let loose.

I always assume everyone has the benefit of being raised in the sticks. I sometimes forget my suburbanite friends have probably never had the opportunity to hone their wilderness bowel movement skills. I am also somewhat surprised at the amount of anxiety some people feel at the thought of dropping a deuce outside the friendly confines of the vertical plastic coffins neatly lined up at the start line of races.

My first bit of advice- *practice*. Don't wait until race day to attempt a torpedo launch in the woods. Next time you're out on the trails, find a secluded spot and give it a go.

So how do you actually go about jettisoning some excess weight?

26

1   **It's all about timing.** Don't try too early. The squatting position you'll adopt is difficult to maintain for more than a minute or two.
2   **Get off the trail.** Twenty feet is usually the minimum. Stay away from water sources. If possible, move out of the line of sight and down-wind of others. It's the courteous thing to do.
3   **Secure your wiping material beforehand.** Any paper will do, as will a bandana or sock. If those items aren't available or you're a staunch conservationist, try leaves, pine cones, sticks, or flat rocks.
4   **If possible, dig a small six inch by six inch hole, perhaps three to four inches deep.** This will be the poo hole.
5   **When pulling down your pants, make sure they're clear of the path the poo will take from butt to ground.** It's the same deal with shoes. You don't want to be sideswiped by a butt nugget.
6   **When squatting, use trees or logs for support if needed.** Practice a variety of positions so you will be prepared for a variety of situations.
7   **Drop the deuce.**
8   **DON'T STAND UP RIGHT AWAY!** It will clench your cheeks together, which increases the wiping.
9   **After the wiping is done, cover the poo with a little dirt, then mix it up.** This aids the decomposition process.
10 **Cover the poo/dirt mixture to prevent others from stepping in it.** I also like to disguise the hole to maintain that "undisturbed nature" look.

Here are some additional pointers:

- When actually squatting, it can be beneficial to hold your cheeks apart. Sadly, I have to credit MTV's *The Real World* for this tip.
- Keeping a small piece of biodegradable toilet paper in your pocket can help with the final cleanup procedure.
- When choosing a location to squat, most people simply wander a fair distance from the trail. Make sure you don't inadvertently walk too close to a different trail or road.
- Know what the local poisonous plants are... don't squat in them. I knew an ultrarunner that squatted in some poison oak. Damn near rectum!
- Avoid plants with thorns, too.
- Same deal with bees.

What to Drink

When it comes to hydration, there are a ton of usable options. I'll run down the list in order of relative popularity.

- **Sports drinks:** This includes products like Gatorade, Heed, Nuun, GU Brew, etc. Most sports drinks provide electrolytes which are lost via sweat. Most also contain varying amounts of calories, which help you stay fueled. In most races, sports drinks are my preferred option, though I sometimes switch to water toward the end. The sweetness of sports drinks sometimes makes me nauseous.
- **Water:** Many people prefer good 'ole water during a race. Water doesn't provide electrolytes or calories, but is palatable throughout a race.
- **Soda:** Not many people use soda, but it does contain calories and some sodium. The carbonation can make it more palatable. If the soda is caffeinated, it may cause a slight diuretic effect. I'll toss energy drinks into this category, too, though the high caffeine levels make it impractical for a primary hydration strategy. Unless you're a crack addict.
- **Juice:** Juice is actually a pretty good option and was more popular before the widespread use of sports drinks. It tends to be relatively high in caloric content, but also has a heavy flavor.
- **Beer/ Wine/ other Alcohol:** I've experimented with both beer and wine, and once did an unfortunate "tequila run." The result of all three was roughly the same: it sucked. The bitterness of beer seemed to be enhanced the longer I ran, which ruled out any good beer. I tried drinking beers like Michelob Ultra, but I had a hard time distinguishing it from water. Wine was okay, but I needed to drink too much to remain relatively well hydrated. Drunkenness inhibits trail running. Go figure.

Jesse Scott enjoying a high altitude energy drink

Food

Running burns energy... *a lot* of energy. Most people burn somewhere around 100 to 130 calories per mile traveled. Over the course of an ultra or long trail run, that adds up to at least tens of thousands of calories. As I prepare for an ultra, I like to get an idea of how much food I will need to consume. I like to simplify this process as much as possible.

Before starting the process, let's look at a few principles. Your body can use two primary fuel sources- fat and carbohydrates. Carbs burn quickly and efficiently. Fat burns slowly. If you're running fast, our body will burn carbs. The slower you run, the more fat our body uses as fuel. The "crashing" feeling you get is the result of making the switch from carb-burning to fat-burning.

You have a limited supply of carbs available at any given time, but you have a HUGE supply of fat. If you want to burn carbs, you need to constantly replace them by consuming calories during the run. This will allow you to run faster. You could get by without eating anything and rely on your fat stores, but you would have to keep intensity to a minimum. It's like the difference between throwing a piece of newspaper on a fire versus a giant oak log- the paper burns quickly with a huge flame while the log burns longer with a much less intense flame.

Through training, I know I can run about 18 miles before my carbohydrate supply is exhausted. At that point, my body switches to fat-burning mode I slow down considerably and experience a crash. I can calculate a ballpark estimate of the carbs I have to consume during the run to avoid that crash by subtracting 18 from the total miles of the race, then multiplying that number by 100.

50 miles - 18 miles = 32
32 * 100 = 3,200 calories needed during the run to avoid the crash

During a 50 miler, I know I have to consume approximately 3,200 calories. This is where it gets a little tricky. Most people can only digest about 200-300 calories per hour. Let's assume you can process 250 calories per hour. If you're running at a 12 minute/mile pace (for a 10 hour finish), you could consume 2,500 calories during that 10 hour race. Since you need 3,200, you won't be able to consume enough to avoid a crash.

The problem becomes more pronounced with longer races. How about a 100 miler?

10 miles – 18miles = 82
82 * 100 = 8,200 calories needed during the run to avoid the crash

This is what I do to remedy the situation:

1. Train to eat. I've managed to get to the point where I can comfortably eat up to 500 calories per hour when running, which allows me to keep fueling throughout most races.
2. Train to burn fat. This is the idea behind the Maffetone method discussed at various points later in the book. This is also the reason I occasionally do long runs after fasting for 24 hours.
3. Start consuming calories from the beginning of a race. The longer you wait, the less opportunity you have to stay ahead of the carb game.
4. Find foods that are palatable even after running long distances. I have at least four "backup foods" in case the aid station foods aren't cutting it.

5. **Know what the "crash" feels like.** When it starts to hit, slow down and consume something sweet.

Food before a Run

Through extensive experimentation, I've managed to find a handful of foods that work well as a pre-run meal. The criteria is straight-forward: The food has to be easy to digest and give me plenty of energy that will last for a relatively long time, yet still be relatively "digestible."

My preferred foods, in order of preference, are:

- Pop Tarts (frosted strawberry, the only *real* Pop Tart flavor)
- Muffins
- Miniature Donuts

As you can tell, I'm a fan of sweet pastries.

To figure out which foods work best, test a different food before each run. I would recommend giving a food at least two opportunities as results can be influenced by other factors.

Some other popular foods include:

- Fruit
- Oatmeal
- Breakfast cereal
- Pancakes
- French toast
- Anything from the breakfast menu at McDonald's

There are some foods to avoid, namely spicy foods. Good rule of thumb- if it's hot going in, it's going to be hotter going out. The "burning ring of fire" atomic anal sphincter can be a major distraction.

Food during a Run

Fueling during a run can be difficult logistically, so I would recommend taking two approaches:

1. Train using food typically found at ultra aid stations, like candy, chips, boiled potatoes, cookies, soda, peanut butter and jelly sandwiches, or any specific food a goal race advertises. This will allow you to use aid stations for fueling if necessary. I prefer to use my own food, but I have run into situations when it wasn't available. Learning to fuel off what is available can solve a lot of potential problems.

2. **Find foods that work well for you.** This includes foods that are easy to carry, can be stuffed in drop bags, or can be carried by your crew. Since many ultras are run far from civilization, non-perishable foods that require little or no preparation would be ideal. Also, your palate will change throughout a race. What tastes good at mile five probably won't taste good at mile 35 or mile 95. Test different foods at different distances.

Food after a Run

"Recovery" food has become a bit of an interesting topic in the running world. Conventional wisdom that existed for decades suggested eating a carbohydrate-rich meal within 90 minutes of running to replace the carbs lost during the run. A few runners have been advocating different approaches ranging from high protein (the paleo crowd) to fruits (fruitarians) to fasting (supermodels.)

In my own experimentation, I found virtually no effect with any of these approaches. While some are backed by a study or two, no approach really accounts for the variability that exists in humans.

My logical solution- *eat based on cravings*. If you're hungry eat. If not, don't. If steak   soundsgood, eat steak. If ice cream sandwiches sound good, eat ice cream sandwiches. Same deal with beer, avocados, or Cheerios.

Pay attention to the effects of various foods. Eventually you will probably notice a pattern. Certain foods will make you feel better the rest of the day. Some foods may help you on your next run. When you find something that works, stick with it.

Clothing

While I'm a proponent of naked running (give it a shot sometime), society dictates we wear clothing most of the time. I've experimented with all kinds of clothing ranging from simple cotton shorts and t-shirts acquired from Goodwill to the latest scientifically-developed technical clothing.

Conditions dictate clothing choice. The clothes used for hot, dry weather will obviously be different than overnight runs in freezing, windy conditions. Your own experimentation will help you make the appropriate choices, but here are a few general guidelines:

- **In cold weather, layers are desirable.** The heat generated via muscle contractions should keep you warm. Stopping is troublesome once you get sweaty. As the sweat evaporates, your body cools rapidly. A moisture-wicking underlayer helps draw sweat away from the body, which helps keep you relatively dry. In very cold weather, I like to use a cotton middle layer. This adds warmth without unnecessary bulk. Finally, a wind and/or waterproof but breathable outer layer will provide a barrier against the elements. Generally speaking, the "technology" of advanced fabrics is a waste of money. Cold weather gear is an exception. The new stuff really is worth the money.

- **In hot weather, less is more.** The human body is especially well-developed for hot weather running as long as sweat is allowed to evaporate from our skin. Many runners like to use moisture-wicking clothing in hot weather, which is a mistake discussed in the "Thermoregulation" section later in the book. The more bare skin you can expose, the better. There IS an exception to this, however. If you're running in an area with a lot of direct sunlight (like Death Valley), wearing white clothing will reflect more heat than your darker skin.

- **Alternative choices.** Some clothing may seem like a weird option but works really well. For example, I experimented endlessly with kilts. They allowed me to go commando, which kept my junk cooler and drier and also cut down on salt deposit-induced chafing. I also found wide-brimmed straw gardening hats worked well in hot weather. They're lightweight, sweat-proof, allow sweat on the head to evaporate, reflect heat from above, and shade the upper torso. Finally, I found cotton pajama pants to be ideal nighttime running pants. The thin cotton was breathable but still provided a degree of insulation.

Gear

Every piece of gear you carry should serve a specific purpose based on the worst case scenario you'll face. If you're running in an urban park with a group of friends, there's no need for survival gear. Leave the fire starter and snake bite kit at home. If you're running on backcountry trails in colder weather, you should carry gear that will allow you to survive in the event something catastrophic occurs.

It is also important to know how to use all of your gear. A GPS watch or emergency beacon is of little use if you don't know how to use it. It's also useful to understand all of the *potential* uses for your gear. For example, a bandana is usually used to shade the head or neck. It can also be used to cool the body when wet, cover the face during a sandstorm or heavy winds, filter sediment from water or extract water from mud, can be used as a tourniquet, can be shredded and used as a fire starter, can be cut into lengths and braided into rope, or used to wipe your ass if you have to drop a deuce. All gear has the potential for multiple uses, and knowing those uses will reduce the amount of gear that must be carried into the field.

A random selection of ultra gear

Trekking Poles

Trekking poles are popular among mountain trail runners. They provide extra leverage when ascending and support when descending. They can also be used to help prevent falls.

Personally I hate trekking poles because they're difficult to use in conjunction with handheld water bottles. I also don't like carrying poles on flat sections of the trail.

If you do a lot of mountain trail running, borrow a pair and try them on a few runs. You may love them. Or hate them. Or find they're well-suited for specific conditions.

Shoes

The shoes you choose to wear for trail running should reflect the conditions and terrain you'll encounter. Some conditions may warrant heavy, durable shoes with aggressive tread and a sturdy rock plate (hard piece of plastic embedded in the sole of the shoe to protect the foot from sharp rocks). On non-technical or even moderately technical trails, road running shoes or even minimalist shoes can be used. With practice, many of those trails could be run barefoot.

So how do you go about choosing shoes? I weigh these variables:

- **Tread**: The tread of the shoe refers to the knobs on the bottom of the sole. This is what grips the terrain. Large, prominent knobs, much like cleats, will be useful in loose dirt, sand, or muddy conditions. Smaller knobs with less space between are useful for harder surfaces. For bare rock or very hard trails, there's no need for a knobbed tread. The composition of the rubber used for the sole is also significant. Some compounds are "stickier" than others and will grip rocks better than harder compounds. The tradeoff is usually durability- softer, stickier compounds wear faster than the harder compounds.
- **Sole Protection**: The stack height, or thickness of the sole, will determine how much protection the shoe provides. A thicker sole will provide more protection. As mentioned above, the presence of a rock plate also adds protection. The more technical the trail, the more protection is needed and the thicker the sole must be. The tradeoff is ground feel and proprioception. "Ground feel" is the ability to feel the terrain under foot. Many people prefer as minimal a shoe as possible, as it helps traverse difficult terrain. Proprioception is our awareness of body position. A thinner sole allows for better proprioception. This helps prevent injuries like sprained ankles.

- **Cushioning:** Cushioning refers to the "give" of the shoe under foot. A shoe with more cushioning has more of a marshmallow feel, whereas a shoe with less cushioning will feel harder. Cushioning can provide additional comfort when running longer distances. The tradeoff is efficiency- the more cushioning under foot, the less "springiness" the legs have. That loss of springiness may have a negative impact on efficiency.

- **Heel Drop:** Heel drop refers to the difference in stack height as measured in the center of the heel and the center of the area under the ball of the foot. The drop is usually measured in millimeters expressed as "8 mm drop." The vast majority of shoes either have a 'zero-drop" heel where the measurements are the same or have a slightly raised heel. Raising the heel will affect posture, which may cause unnecessary stresses on the lower back and knees. Because of this, I prefer shoes with 4 mm drop or less. Shoes that have a greater drop alter your posture just like a stripper wearing 4" stilettos. They cause your chest and ass stick out. Cool effect for the stage... not so much out on the trails.

- **Upper:** The upper is the top part of the shoe that encases the foot. Uppers are chosen based on comfort and conditions. Some shoes have a softer, more flexible upper. This adds to comfort, but may cause the shoe to move around on the foot. This is especially problematic when running downhill. Stiffer uppers help secure the shoe to the foot, but may not be as comfortable. Many uppers are now being designed with little or no internal seams so they can be worn without socks. Some uppers are made to resist water for use in rainy weather or trails with many water crossings. Others are designed with insulation for cold weather running. Choose the shoe that appropriately matches the conditions.

- **Ventilation:** Ventilation refers to the breathability of the shoe, or the ability for air circulation. Greater ventilation keeps your feet cool and dry. It also allows debris like dust and sand to enter the shoe.
- **Shape of last:** The "last' is the device used to mold the shoe during the manufacturing process. Different manufacturers use different lasts, and many manufacturers use multiple lasts. Last shape tends to be a matter of personal preference. I prefer an "anatomical last" that conforms to the shape of the human foot. This reduces the rubbing between my foot and the inside of the shoe, which allows me to run sockless without blistering. My best advice- try several brands and models of shoes until you find a last you prefer.

Carrying Water

Most people use one of three options for carrying water or sports drinks. They use handheld water bottles, hydration packs that are affixed to the back, or complicated fanny packs that carry water bottles. Each one has pros and cons.

Handhelds: Handhelds have three major advantages. Having your drink in your hands helps you remember to drink regularly, offers some hand protection should you fall, and are easy to fill at aid stations. The downside to handhelds is weight. It can be difficult to carry a 20 to 24 ounce water bottle all day. Also, I've had some problems with the strap on the water bottle chafing my knuckles.

Hydration packs: Hydration packs hold far more of your favorite beverage than handhelds, and the weight is equally distributed on your back. The backpacks can bounce around if your running form is too "bouncy" (see the section on good form). Hydration packs are also a pain in the ass to fill at aid stations, though you have to fill them less often.

Fanny packs: In my opinion, these are the worst of both worlds. The water bottles are held around your butt, which requires reaching back to grab. Since the bottles are out of sight, there's no reminder to drink. Finally, the pack itself may cause chafing due to bouncing.

It is possible to run without anything and just rely on the aid stations. I wouldn't advise this if you are a new ultrarunner, especially if it is hot or the aid stations are farther than five miles apart.

Knowing Where to Find Water

When it comes to training, hydration can be a bitch. Once the long runs surpass your ability to physically carry enough water (or other drink), your options are limited. You can:

- Stash drinks along the planned route in some sort of jug or container (though they may get stolen... which has happened on more than one occasion. Seriously, who steals a jug of water?!? Fucking rednecks!) A related option is to plan a loop route that will take you back to your vehicle.
- Bring money or a credit card if there will be stores along the way.
- Plan a route that utilizes public drinking fountains.

Personally, I prefer the last option. If you live in a semi-inhabited area, this is a good option. If you live in the sticks or will be training in desolate mountains, it may be impossible. If you do train in a populated area, drinking fountains can usually be found at:

- Public parks and playgrounds
- Sport fields
- Public restrooms
- Schools
- Trailheads
- Campgrounds
- Large grocery, department, or other such stores
- Malls

Water from Natural Sources

You're out on a long run and your bottle goes dry. You start experiencing the early signs of dehydration. You are nowhere near a drinking fountain or a store. What do you do?

I've run into this scenario many times over the years... and I always choose the same course of action- I scavenge for water anywhere I can. That has included drinking from streams, lakes, a water hose in some random person's yard, or making a funnel out of a leaf during a rainstorm.

There's always an inherent danger in drinking water from questionable sources. The water may contain organisms that can make you sick, like giardia or dysentery. The water could also be contaminated with poisons that could kill you. It's always a gamble.

In an emergency situation, I look for water that contains some form of life. If a water source does not have any signs of life (fish, plants, etc.), odds are pretty good that it's undrinkable. Next, I make a filter out of a bandana and a water bottle by placing the bandana over the mouth of the bottle and attaching it with rubber bands (I keep a few rubber bands wrapped around all my water bottles). When the bottle is submerged, the bandana acts as a filter.

It's not nearly as effective as boiling water, using a commercial filter, or chemically purifying the water, but rarely do I, if ever, have the tools required for elaborate purification. The homemade filter will likely trap most of the harmful stuff and is better than drinking straight from the questionable source.

If you have access to a piece of plastic or a space blanket and a container of some sort, you can make a solar still. A water bottle works well. The setup will use evaporation to purify water over the course of several hours. Here's how to construct the still:

- Dig a hole 18" deep by 24" wide in a sunny area.
- Line the hole with one piece of plastic.
- Place a small rock or mound of dirt in the middle of the plastic.
- Place your container on the mound.
- Dump contaminated water, urine, or green plants in the hole.

41

- Cover the entire hole with another piece of plastic and secure it in place by placing rocks or dirt around the edge. The better the coverage, the better the still will work.
- Place a small pebble on top of the cover sheet directly above the mouth of the container.

How it works: The still works when the sun heats the contaminated water, urine, or plants, which evaporates the water. The evaporated water collects on the bottom of the cover sheet. The pebble in the middle causes the water to run down the sheet and drip in the bottle. If you don't have enough plastic or you have no water or plants to place in the hole, skip the liner from step two. The still will draw moisture from the ground.

If you're near a water source like a river, stream, or a beach and you can build a fire, the process can be expedited. Dig a hole near the water source deep enough so the bottom fills with water. Place a container in the center, and then partially cover the hole with the plastic. Build a fire a few feet from the hole. Place a few rocks in the fire. After a few minutes, use a stick to move the hot rocks into the water hole, then immediately cover the hole with the plastic and drop a pebble above the mouth of the container. After a few minutes, place the rocks back in the fire and repeat.

Water can also be extracted from mud with the use of a sock, bandana, shirt, or other fabric. Wrap a softball-size clump of mud in the fabric

42

(or plop it in the sock). Squeeze the fabric over a container. The fabric will effectively hold most of the dirt behind. The water will still have to be purified, however.

To cool the water (or any other liquid), you can once again utilize fabric. Socks work best. Drop the sealed container of water (or beer cans... whatever) in the sock. Saturate the sock with water. It doesn't have to be purified water. Hang the sock in a shady area exposed to wind. The blowing aids the evaporation of the water, which cools the liquid in the container. I have Jeremiah Cataldo to thank for that tip.

What if there aren't obvious water sources? Remember water always flows downhill. Birds also tend to congregate near water at dawn and dusk. Look for them circling in the sky. Here are some location-specific places that can be used as, or may lead to, sources of water:

- **Cold environments-** snow and ice
- **Desert-** trails, animal droppings, birds, palm trees, base of hills or mountains
- **Forest-** animal trails (get wider and deeper toward water source, downhill), birds, insects, density and "greenness" of plants, if spring bed is dry, dig
- **Mountains-** valleys, crevices in rock (formed by flowing water),
- **Plains-** look for taller vegetation like small trees growing in groups (pond) or a line (stream)

GPS

Global positioning system (GPS) technology is a marvel of the modern world. By using a series of geostationary satellites coupled with receivers here on Earth, we can find our exact location anywhere. It allows us to get directions, track mileage, our route, and our velocity.

The most common devices used by runners are basically wristwatches. They collect data as we move. The data can then be uploaded to a computer for analysis and sharing.

This data can be used for a variety of purposes. I like to know the speed, distance, and elevation change of the routes I run. It also provides a cool compilation of your travels. Shelly and I saved the data from our runs as we traveled the country. This has been useful when recommending specific trails to others.

Most road runners fall in love with their GPS watches because the data can be endlessly analyzed. Trail runners seem to either love them or hate them. The data can be great, but obsessing over your pace or distance may distract you from enjoying the natural surroundings that define trail running.

GPS devices can serve as useful rescue tools for trail runners. If you become lost or injured and have a means of communicating (cell phone, for example), a GPS device can give your exact location, which can be relayed to search and rescue (SAR) personnel. Also, most devices have a "return to start" function which allows you to backtrack your path or return via a direct line. I've had to use this function on more than one occasion when running in unfamiliar areas.

Map and compass

A map and compass are basic necessities for hikers, but most runners leave them at home. A decent topographical map and compass take up a lot of room. Furthermore, most runners simply rely on knowledge of the area or trail markings for navigation.

But what if you're venturing into unknown or poorly-marked areas? Carrying a map and compass becomes a critical necessity. Getting lost in the backcountry is not only dangerous, but it taxes rescue resources and puts others at risk. It tends to be expensive, too.

The first step is acquiring the right map. The best maps tend to be topographical maps produced by the U.S. Geological Society (USGS) or private companies that produce more detailed maps based off the USGS maps. They will list most trails, roads, water, and have accurate elevation profiles denoted with shading and contour lines. These maps can be purchased at local outdoor stores or bookstores. The maps are easy to decipher with the legend.

Any basic compass can be used to determine magnetic north. This, in conjunction with an accurate map, can be used to determine your location on most maps by comparing your surroundings to the landforms on the map. This VERY rudimentary method is about as advanced as I get when using a map and compass in the field.

For those that are more detail-oriented, a good map and compass can be used for very intricate navigation, including adjusting for the difference between magnetic and true north, navigating from one landmark to another, and finding your exact location using triangulation from visible landmarks. The exact details of these skills goes beyond the scope of this book, but are easy to learn via the Interwebz or classes offered by companies like REI.

In other words, most trail runners don't give a damn about learning intricate navigation skills and carrying the requisite tools. *We're stupid that way.*

Natural Navigation Aids

In the event you don't have a compass and map, it's still possible to ascertain direction using a few natural methods, including:

- **The sun:** It rises in the east and sets in the west. It doesn't get much more basic than that.
- **Stick shadow method:** Place a stick in the ground, then stick a pebble at the end of the shadow. Wait about 30 minutes. Place another pebble at the end of the second shadow. Draw a line between the pebbles. The first pebble is west, the second is east. North is perpendicular to the line in the direction away from the sticks.
- **North star:** In the Northern Hemisphere, you can find north by locating the North Star. Look for the Big Dipper constellation. The far edge of the ladle (the right end of the constellation) points toward the North Star, which is five times the distance from the edge of the ladle to the North Star.
- **Snow:** Snow will melt from the southern-facing slopes first.
- **Moss:** This tends to be unreliable, but moss usually grows more on the shadowy north side of any object.
- **Satellite dishes:** Okay, this isn't quite "natural", but nonetheless effective. If you see a house with a satellite dish, the dish will always point south.

Cell Phones

If you are running in an area with reception, a cell phone can be a potential lifesaver.

Get lost? Call Search and Rescue.
Get hurt? Call for an extraction.
Get bored? Play Angry Birds.

However, cell phones are only effective if your battery lasts throughout the trip and you're in a place with adequate reception. Many remote trails in the United States are far from cell towers, so phones are useless. There are products on the market like boosters, repeaters, and directional antennas that can be used to increase the range of a cell phone, but they're not practical to carry while running.

Since I tend to run in many areas with poor reception, I rarely carry a phone. If I do, I keep it in "airplane mode" unless needed. If left in regular mode, the phone will actively send out signals to establish a connection with towers in the area, which will drain the battery faster. Thanks to James Barstad for that tip.

Personal Location Beacons

Personal Location Beacons (PLB) are small devices designed to assist search and rescue units by alerting them of an emergency and giving them your location. Some devices (the better choice) use a 406 MHz signal relayed by satellite. Other options, like the SPOT emergency beacon, use similar methods. All devices work by sending a distress signal to a central location where the signal is forwarded to local authorities. When the unit is purchased, a registration is submitted which gives SAR valuable information such as your name, contact phone numbers, etc. Once a signal is received, a rescue team will be dispatched.

Since these devices do not rely on cell phone signals, they can be invaluable in remote locations. The technology is reliable and accurate. The only real down side is false alarms. Many rescue outfits have responded to non-emergency situations (like campers being too cold) which is a monumental waste of resources. If you use a PLB, make sure it's only used in a genuine emergency.

Personal Protection

Sometimes trail running will bring you to dangerous locations. That danger may come from animals or other people. Because of this, some people prefer to carry some sort of personal protection. Some common choices are mace, pepper spray, knives, kubotan (small handheld weapon... my favorite flashlight doubles as a kubotan), or even guns. Never know when you'll wanna cap an ass out in the boonies!

My trusty Fenix

Of these choices, pepper spray would probably be the most effective as a deterrent. Not only could it be used against people, it could also be used against bears, wolves, or mountain lions. The rest of the choices are rather cumbersome, though I do carry a small pocket knife and flashlight on very long backcountry trail runs.

The key to all options is knowing how to use the weapon. In the unlikely event you'll need to use the weapon, you probably won't have much warning. In short, practice with the weapon. Know how to use it and carry it in a way that it can be utilized immediately. Pepper spray doesn't do much good against an attacking grizzly if you have to dig it out of the bottom of your hydration pack.

Both Shelly and I have started training at a mixed martial arts gym, where we're learning boxing, kickboxing, and jiu jitsu fighting techniques. Who knows, they may come in handy if we're attacked on a trail. I doubt we'll be able to choke out a cougar or grizzly bear, but it *does* boost confidence.

Flashlights and Headlamps

If you plan to do any nighttime trail running, illumination of some sort is pretty much a necessity. Some trails can be safely navigated by lighting (like urban parks) or moonlight during a full moon, but most require a light. The options are handheld flashlights or headlamps. If you want to go old school, I suppose you could use a flaming torch. I wouldn't recommend that route in areas prone to wildfires, however.

Many people prefer headlamps. I don't like headlamps because the light is too close to your eyes. The shadows cast by the light are almost impossible to see, which makes it difficult to determine the exact height of debris on the trail. A handheld carried at about waist level casts shadows on a different plane, which makes obstacle discrimination far easier.

My current preference is the Fenix brand of handhelds. They make several models that use standard AA batteries (easy to find), last through the night, are extremely durable, and ridiculously bright. As mentioned earlier, it can also be used as a kubotan in an emergency. My preferred model throws 190 lumens, which more or less turns the night to day. The light is so bright it can even turn some fabrics transparent... or so I'm told.

In the event you're ever stranded on the trail in darkness and have no light, you can easily enhance your night vision. First, don't move during civil twilight, or the point where all light disappears from the sky. It takes about 30 minutes for your eyes to fully adjust to the darkness. When your eyes adjust to the darkness, look to the side of an object you're looking at. Our eyes are made up of cells called rods and cones. Rods are primarily responsible for low light vision and have a higher concentration in the parts of our eyes that register peripheral vision. At night, you can't see an object quite as well if you look directly at it.

Familiarity with Local Weather Patterns

Pretty much everywhere Shelly and travel, we encounter the phrase, "If you don't like the weather here in [insert state here], wait 15 minutes." While it's true some areas of the country have truly unpredictable weather, most weather patterns can be divined hours or even days ahead of time.

As a general rule, weather patterns in North America usually move from west to east. Look west. Whatever weather you see will hit you in the near future.

Temperature and humidity (along with a few other factors) can be used in conjunction with the time of year to get a reliable snapshot of possible weather patterns.

As an example, late afternoon thunderstorms during the hot summer days are a predictable pattern for the Colorado Rocky Mountains. If you're familiar with that almost daily occurrence, you'll avoid summiting mountains in the afternoon (unlike Shelly and I when we summited a 14er just as the afternoon thunderstorms developed... took days to clean my shorts).

Before running in a new area, take a few minutes to check local hiking guides or the local weather service's website. They will give you tips on the expected weather conditions for that season.

Checking the Weather Forecast

Once you're familiar with local weather patterns, you'll know what you can reasonably expect as a worst-case scenario. Checking the immediate forecast will give you exact details of what to expect. Well, as exact as meteorology can be.

Prior to any running excursion, I'll check wunderground.com and at least one local news outlet to get the weather forecast. I look at the hourly forecasts to determine temperatures and the likelihood of precipitation. I also look at the five day forecast and pay special attention to overnight low temperatures. In the unlikely event I get lost and am forced to spend a night or two in the wilderness, I like to know just how bad it will get. *This forecast always dictates the gear and clothing I'll carry.*

Natural Weather Predictors

Learning natural weather predictors is a great tool to add to your repertoire of knowledge. If you forget to check the local forecast, nature provides more than enough clues to predict the weather hours or even days before the shit hits the fan.

Clouds

Clouds are among the most reliable predictors of weather... mostly because they are the source of precipitation. Here are the common types:

- **Cirrostratus-** these high, wispy clouds are a sign of good weather in the immediate future, but precipitation may be on the way in 12 to 24 hours.
- **Stratocumulus-** These clouds appear as big lumpy clouds that cover most of the sky.. They generally indicate no weather change in the near future.
- **Cumulonimbus-** These are the giant, tall clouds that look a little bit like an anvil. These clouds are bad. They produce thunderstorms. If you see them approaching, seek cover.
- **Stratus-** These clouds form an even sheet across the entire sky. They usually produce long-lasting light rain or drizzle.
- **Cumulus-** These are the clouds that look like cotton balls. If they're spread far apart and are relatively small. They represent fair weather. If they are beginning to grow in size vertically, that's an indicator of approaching storms.

Red Sky...

"Red sky at night, sailors' delight. Red sky in the morning, sailors take warning."

I first heard this saying on the elementary school playground in second grade. I thought it was dumb. How could the color of the sky actually predict rain? As it turns out, the saying is a moderately accurate measure of upcoming weather, as long as you're not in the tropics or polar circles. I took a weather class as a freshman at Central Michigan University. The prof gave a lengthy explanation of the phenomenon.

The concept is based on particles in the air. The setting sun turns the westerly sky red at sunset if there's a lot of dust particles in the air, which is synonymous with high pressure. High pressure usually indicated calm weather. Since weather systems generally move west to east, the high pressure will predominate the following day. It could also be caused by a lack of westerly clouds in the sky (since the clouds would block out the sunset).

The red sky in the morning phenomenon is attributed to a few things. First, it could be high particle content from an already-passed system, which means low pressure is near. It could also be caused by clear skies to the east, which is an indicator or an already-passed high pressure system.

Calm before the Storm

Sometimes violent weather can be preceded by an eerie "calm" where the wind dies down and everything seems to get quiet. This occasional phenomenon is a bad sign- a storm is imminent. Not all storms produce this calm period, so don't use this as your lone predictive method.

The "calm" is caused by a vacuum created when a storm sucks warm, moist air into the center of the low pressure cell. This "sucking" can suck air from all directions, including ahead of the storm. As the air circulates through the clouds, moisture is removed as temperatures drop. The now dry, stable air spills out over the storm and back to your location. The result is the calm before the storm.

The problem with this predictor is timing- it usually occurs within 5-15 minutes before a storm hits. In fact, it's common to hear the rumble of thunder or see the storm clouds to the west well before you experience the calm. By the time you feel the calm, you have precious little time to take cover.

Pine Cones

Pine cones are nature's hygrometer. In humid conditions, pine cones expand. In dry conditions, they contract. Generally speaking, high humidity precedes wet weather, and low humidity precedes dry weather.

Wind Direction

Wind direction can be used to predict weather patterns. If there's a westerly wind, there's a good chance the weather is going to be fair. If there's an easterly wind, it's a sign the weather is about to change for the worst.

This one has to do with the nature of low-pressure systems, which are associated with storms. The low pressure system swirls counter-clockwise. As it approaches an area, this counter-clockwise rotation causes the wind to shift from the west to the east.

Cows

When I was a kid, I grew up in close proximity to a dairy farm. I spent a good portion of my youth around cows. It was magical. If you happen to have access to cows, they can be used as a makeshift weathervane. Cows have a weird peculiarity- they prefer to have wind blowing at their ass versus their head. As such, they tend to stand away from the prevailing wind.

Based on the idea above, if cows are facing east, expect good weather. If cows are facing west, expect bad weather. Weird, huh?

Campfires

When a high-pressure system is present, the air is stable. When a low-pressure system is present, the air is turbulent. If you build a campfire, the behavior of the smoke can indicate high or low pressure.

If the smoke rises straight up or is carried in one direction, it's likely due to the stability of high pressure. Expect good weather in the near future.

If the smoke swirls unpredictably, it's likely due to the turbulence of low pressure. Expect bad weather.

Frizzy or Curly Hair

Hair out of control? It could be the result of high humidity, which is a sign of precipitation in the near future. I have Shelly to thank for this one. As we travel, we routinely visit areas with higher or lower humidity. She'll often comment about the effects of the area on her hair. The key is waiting for her hair to suddenly get curly in an area where it was otherwise relatively flat. That's a sign rain is in the forecast.

Bugs

In many areas, insects can be used to predict weather. I find ants to be among the most reliable. If rain is near, ants tend to flee back to their nests. If you see a lot of ants moving in the same direction, it's probably going to rain soon. Ants also build the domes at the entrance to their nests higher and will cap them off prior to rain.

Biting insects usually bite more often immediately prior to rain. In Michigan, we could predict rain by the increased aggressiveness of black flies (late spring) and deer flies (summer). I've been told the same rules apply in other geographic areas.

Dew on Grass

If there's dew on the grass in the morning, it's a good sign fair weather is in the immediate forecast. If the grass is dry, expect precipitation. This concept has to do with wind. Dew only forms in relatively calm conditions associated with high pressure. If there's a low-pressure front approaching, the winds will pick up and prevent dew from forming.

Speaking of dew- if you ever need an emergency water source, drag a piece of fabric over dew-covered grass then wring out over a container.

Jet Tails

Jet tails are the trails left by jets as they pass overhead. Jet tails normally dissipate within a minute or so. Higher moisture content in the air will increase their longevity. If they last significantly longer, there could be precipitation within a day.

Moon Rings

"Rings" that appear around the moon can also be used to predict weather. The rings are caused by high-altitude ice particles, which precede precipitation.

What to do in a Severe Thunderstorm

In the event you're stuck outdoors in a severe storm, a few steps will keep you safe. The key is to protect yourself from lightning, flood waters, and hail.

First, know when to seek cover. The distance of an approaching storm can be determined by the differential between seeing the light of the lightning and hearing the sound of the thunder. Count the number of seconds between the lightning and thunder, then divide by five. That will give you the distance in miles. If you're more of a metric system fan, divide by three for kilometers.

Since lightning can strike miles ahead of the storm clouds, you should seek cover when the lightning and thunder are separated by 30 seconds or less.

If you're in an open area or a place with a variety of elevations, move away from high ground. Get off summits and ridges. However, don't go too low. Low areas are prone to flash flooding, so avoid the bottom of valleys or channels. You can usually determine floodplains by a noticeable debris line. Stay away from lone trees or other tall, solitary objects. If you're in a group, separate by at least 25 feet. This will prevent the entire group from being struck by a single lightning strike.

Hail can be dangerous if it's larger than a dime. If it begins to hail, take cover under a sturdy object like a cave, rock outcropping, or a fallen tree. If you don't have sturdy cover, drop to your knees, place your head near the ground, and cover it with your hands or any other object you're carrying. The goal is to avoid head trauma.

Dangerous Fauna

Sometimes trail runners encounter animals. Sometimes those animals can hurt you. Most are easy to handle... *if you know how to react.* Here's a rundown of the most common animals encountered in North America.

Snakes

Before running in a new area, learn to identify the native poisonous snakes. Should you encounter one on the trail, avoid it. Furthermore, avoid putting your hands and feet in areas you cannot see. As a general rule, snakes can strike better when coiled versus stretched across the trail.

If you are bitten, stay in one place if others will be passing (like a race.) Otherwise, get to safety as quickly as possible. Evacuation via helicopter or motor vehicle is best, followed by walking. Running will cause your heart to beat faster, which circulates the venom faster. Restrict movement as much as possible, which can include splinting the affected area. Try to identify the snake, but don't risk others being bit. If it helps, only a fraction of one percent of snakebite victims actually die from the bite.

Spiders and Scorpions

Spiders and scorpions present many of the same dangers as snakes-they may be venomous. Learn to identify the really dangerous species in your area. If you are bit or stung, follow the same guidelines.

A major difference between snakes and spiders/scorpions has to do with clothing- spiders and scorpions may crawl into your clothing or shoes and will bite you when dressing. It's good to get in the habit of shaking out your clothing and shoes before putting them on.

Bees and wasps

Bees and wasps aren't usually as dangerous... unless you have an allergy to their venom. If you ARE allergic to bee venom, it's a good idea to carry an epinephrine pen when trail running.

If you are stung, escape the area. Avoid that particular area as the bees or wasps will probably be agitated. Odds are good you disrupted their nest. If the stinger is stuck in your skin, scrape it off with your fingernail.

While running the Burning River 100 miler a few years ago, I stepped on a wasp nest. I was only stung once on the heel (I was wearing huarache sandals.) The next ten miles sucked before the pain dissipated, but I was lucky. I was wearing a kilt for the race. The thoughts of getting stung in the junk was enough to dissuade me from wearing a kilt for any future trail race.

Ticks

Ticks are mostly a problem on the East Coast, where they're known to carry Lyme disease. To avoid ticks, stay on the trail. Avoid long grass immediately off the trail. If you find a tick attached to your skin, remove it with tweezers, wash with soap, and apply antiseptic to the area.

Bears

Most bears in the United States will avoid contact with humans unless they're protecting cubs, territory, or they feel you're threatening their food supply. If you do encounter a bear and they aren't aware of your presence, back away slowly. If they are aware of your presence, make some noise and talk in a low voice. Avoid eye contact. The goal is to identify yourself as a human. The bear will probably try to avoid you.

If a bear does attack, don't run. They have no problem outrunning a human. The only situation where running is advisable- Your running partner is both annoying *and* slower than you. Otherwise, climb a high tree if possible. Note: black bears are good climbers. Unless you can get to branches that will support your weight but not their weight, climbing is futile.

If you have pepper spray, this is the time to use it. Spray it before the bear actually reaches you.

If they make physical contact, you're in trouble. There are two schools of thought- fight back or play dead. Since many bear attacks are defensive in nature, they will stop when they believe the threat has been neutralized. Personally, I'd play dead. If you DO decide to fight back, having a weapon helps.

Moose, Elk, and Deer

Most people don't concern themselves with these seemingly peace-loving herbivores. However, they can and will attack humans and are capable of killing.

Like with bears, keep your distance. Announce your presence. If they charge, get behind cover to separate yourself from them. Trees or large rocks work well. If they do reach you, fall to the ground, cover your head, and play dead. They will probably stop stomping you once they believe the threat is neutralized.

Cougars

Cougars, at least in the Western United States, present a real threat. They are adept predators. They have an uncanny ability to stalk their prey. Once they determine you're a target, you're essentially powerless. The trick is to be able to identify their presence. In my experience, the easiest way to detect cougars is the smell of their perfume and the clicking of their high heels.

Older women preying on younger men aside, mountain lions can be scary because their presence will rarely be known until they're actually attacking you. If you do see a mountain lion, make eye contact. Raise your arms. Appear as big as possible. Make noise. Act aggressive. The big cat is looking for an easy kill, not a protracted fight.

If they *do* attack, don't turn your back. If you have children with you, pick them up. If you value your kids, it will protect them from the cougar's attach. If you don't, they make handy, though noisy, shields.

Use sticks, rocks, running gear, or your fists as weapons. Aim for their eyes, nose, or throat. The goal is to convince the cougar you're a threat and not worth the fight.

Stretching and Rolling

Should you stretch before a run? How about after? What's the deal with foam rollers and that "stick" thingy?

All of these are legitimate questions. And science doesn't really give conclusive answers.

I personally do not stretch. I occasionally use a rolling pin (in place of the expensive rollers you can buy from running stores) if I have an especially tight muscle. Instead of stretching, I prefer to warm up by doing whatever activity I'm about to do. For example, before running I walk for a few minutes, and then progress to a short, slow run. For ultras, I may just start the race with a walk.

I used to do extensive stretching before and after running, but I didn't see a significant benefit. It just took up more time.

I would recommend, like everything else, experimentation. Find a good stretching or rolling routine, do it for a few weeks, and see how you feel. If it improves performance, recovery, or you find it to be enjoyable, keep at it. If it doesn't do anything for you, drop it.

Oh, and the "Stick?" It's just a ridiculously expensive rolling pin designed to separate yuppies from their hard-earned cash. Buy a $5 rolling pin at your local department store, then spend the rest on a race entry.

Learning to Fall

Huh? Isn't falling, by definition, something you can't predict?

Yes. But you can develop your ability to fall *better*.

Falling while trail running is inevitable. Most people do their best to avoid falling and hope they don't get hurt too badly if the unfortunate happens. I'm clumsy. I don't like to take those chances.

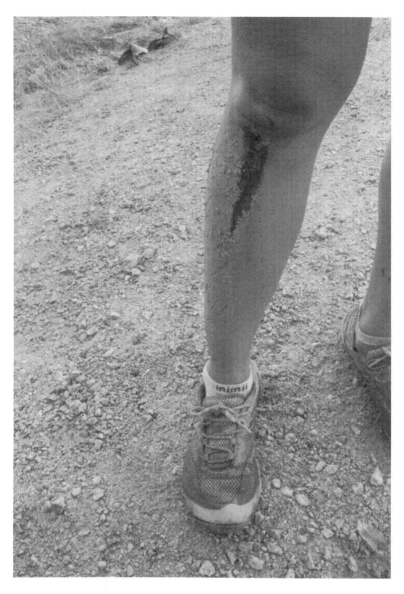

So how do you go about learning to fall?

Find a location with soft ground. Sand is perfect. Grassy fields are another good choice. Run at a slow speed, then purposely fall on the ground. I prefer to use a "slow your fall with your arms, then roll" technique. As you're falling, keep your elbows bent. When you hit the ground with your hands, the bent elbows will act as shock absorbers. Locked elbows can cause a "FOOSH" injury- falling on out-stretched hands. The impact can shatter all bones of the arm, which is not pretty. As my arms are absorbing the shock, I begin rolling my body to the side away from the most dangerous debris. Depending on the trail, I may roll several times.

This specific technique will not work on all trails. For example, it may be impossible to avoid serious injury if falling on rocky mountain trails. In that case, do what you can to avoid smacking your head on a sharp rock. PROTECT YOUR HEAD AT ALL COSTS!

I prefer to carry handheld water bottles to help soften the blow of landing hard on my hands. The bottles usually take a beating, but it saves my hands. Wearing gloves can also serve the same purpose, but may be too hot depending on the weather.

Falling Off a Cliff

Full disclaimer- I've never fallen off a cliff. However, I have run in many environments where it was a distinct possibility. A few years ago, I met a dude on a trail that gave me some "OH SHIT!" advice. That included what to do if you fall off a cliff.

The trick to falling is learning to land in a way that dissipates as much energy as possible. Try to land on your feet. As soon as you touch the ground, roll forward in a ball. If done correctly, this redirects a significant amount of energy. It's possible to practice the technique by jumping off a raised platform. Start with something low... maybe a foot off the ground and progress to higher platforms as you develop the skill.

If you're sliding down a steep hill, you can usually stop the falling using friction. Roll to your belly and spread your arms and legs.

Preparing For Trouble

What happens if you get lost? Or hurt? For anyone venturing into the wilderness, this is a real possibility. Preparing for trouble can help keep you safe. The more remote the area, the more important good preparation becomes. Follow these simple tips.

Before you leave for your run

ALWAYS tell someone where you are going, when you plan on returning, and who to contact should you fail to return. Exact information could include the trailhead where you will start, the number of people in your running group, gear (food, water, fire-starting equipment, clothing, shelter, etc.), your experience level, maps and compass, and your planned route. All of this information can be used by search and rescue to help plan a search effort.

Give the person an exact time you plan on returning. Give yourself some wiggle room in case you're delayed. Instruct them to attempt to call you first in case you forget to call them. If they don't get a response, give them an emergency contact number based on the area you're running. They will forward all your information to the authorities, which will forward it to the search and rescue agency.

In the event this isn't possible, you can leave a note with the same information in your car at the trailhead. If you don't return, search and rescue will locate and search your car. I've never been a fan of this because I don't want to advertise my whereabouts and return time to prospective thieves. If you do this, leave the note folded on the dashboard.

If the trailhead has a register, fill it out. Search and rescue will also use this to locate you.

Don't pull an Aron Ralston.

If you do get lost or hurt

Knowing how search and rescue operates is useful to maximize their efforts to find you. First, stabilize any injuries and move to a safe place. For example, if you're bleeding, stop it. If you're on top of a summit during a thunderstorm, move to lower ground. If you're in a floodplain during a rain storm, move to higher ground.

63

Second, assess the situation. If there's a very good chance of finding your way out of trouble in a timely manner, a storm is closing in and you don't have a means of building a shelter, or you didn't tell anyone where you're running, try navigating out. If not, stay put. If people are searching for you, moving makes it much more difficult to locate you. Understanding how search and rescue works will greatly increase the chances of being found. This is the process SAR usually uses to locate lost runners.

Search and rescue efforts usually start with teams checking obvious locations in the event you're not really lost, like your tent, car, or home. This is done in the event you didn't have a means (or forgot) to contact the person that reported you missing.

The SAR team begins the actual search by determining your last-known location. They calculate the time that has elapsed since you were last seen and how fast you were likely traveling. Using this data, they can determine the size of the search area.

Before beginning the actual search, the SAR team will post people on roads, trails, and streams or rivers around the boundary of the search area. This serves two purposes. If you're moving, there's a chance you will run into one of the SAR team members. This also helps assure the search area doesn't enlarge over time since it will be unlikely you'll pass by one of the containment team members. This is the reason staying in one place is important- moving out of this search zone will *dramatically* increase the time it takes to find you, since the initial search zone will be thoroughly searched first.

The search team will then dispatch small teams to quickly search the zone. They will check any place people may go when lost or injured such as shelters or caves, or check obviously dangerous places like cliffs. The goal of this stage is to end the search quickly, so the searchers aren't especially thorough.

Shortly after, SAR may dispatch helicopters or airplanes to search from the air. They will look for signs like fires, shelters, or signals and notes left on the ground. They may or may not use heat detecting technology.

SAR may also use signaling methods like whistles, car horns, or yelling. If you hear any of these, attempt to respond. If possible, head toward the signals. It's a good idea to mark your path in some way.

This allows you to return to your shelter if needed and creates a series of clues if SAR stumbled upon your path.

If the initial search is unsuccessful, the SAR team may expand the search zone or, more likely, use a grid search of the area. The team will section off the area, then have searchers thoroughly search each section of the grid for any clue they can find. This is a very slow, manpower-intensive process and usually reserved for times when they are searching for an incapacitated person or a body.

You can greatly increase your chances of being found by following a few guidelines that will assist SAR.

Step one: Get safe. If you're in a dangerous place (possible rock slides, avalanche zone, ridge or summit during a thunderstorm, a flood plane, etc.), move to a safe location. If you're injured, administer appropriate first aid.

Step two: Protect yourself from the elements. The greatest danger in a survival situation is exposure. Heat or cold can kill a human surprisingly fast. If you are close to a known shelter, take refuge there. SAR will likely search those first, so it increases your odds of being found. If not, use whatever you have at your disposal to build a makeshift shelter. If you are prepared, you should have an emergency blanket and some cord. This can be combined with trees, sticks, or other natural elements to build a simple lean-to shelter.

Shelter placement is a tradeoff between visibility and protection. If you built the shelter in an open area, it is more likely to be seen from above. However it also exposes you to the elements. It's probably a better idea to build the shelter near a bare hilltop or clearing, then construct signaling devices in the open areas.

This step should also include building a fire if the weather is colder. A small fire built near the open side of a lean-to with a reflector on the opposite side will provide plenty of warmth.

Step three: Build signals for SAR. Make your presence known. The universal distress signal in the United States is a grouping of three. It may be three signal fires built in a triangle, three piles of rocks or clothing, three blasts from a whistle, etc. The ideal location is an open area that can be seen from a distance such as a bare hilltop or large clearing. Here are a few options for signaling:

- **Signal fires.** The smoke from a fire can be seen in the daytime and the flames can be seen at night. To increase the smokiness, add green pine needles or leaves.
- **Clothing arranged in an "X."** Bright clothing can be seen from a long distance. If you have an abundance, leave a clothing "X" in a clearing near your shelter.
- **Signal mirror.** I don't usually carry a mirror when running, but they are a great signal device.
- **Rocks, logs, or dirt arranged in the shape of messages.** Use whatever you have available to create notes in open areas. Write the letters "SOS" if possible, otherwise arrange three piles in a straight line or a triangle. If you move, also include an arrow pointing toward your direction of travel.
- **If you see or hear an aircraft, find an open area and *lie flat on the ground* with your arms and legs spread.** The goal is to be as noticeable as possible.

Step four: Procure water. After exposure, dehydration is the next danger. Humans can live about three days without water. If you have water, use that. Some people recommend rationing, others suggest drinking normally. There are merits to both approaches. I prefer to ration because it's psychologically demoralizing to run out of water. Regardless of the approach, it's important to avoid heavy exertion. Sweating wastes water.

I discuss methods to find water in an earlier section, including methods to purify potentially dangerous water. Drinking untreated water has risks ranging from illness to death. If you've exhausted your water and are in danger of dehydration, it may be worth the risk of drinking untreated water. Most illnesses may take a week or more before symptoms show up. If people are searching for you and you followed all the advice in here, you'll be found before it becomes an issue.

Step five: Find food. Food is the last step because humans can survive for weeks without food. While it may seem like an immediate concern, the other steps are FAR more important. If you're trapped in the wilderness long enough to starve, you probably didn't tell someone when or where you were running. Even then, it's unlikely that you would have remained missing.

If you DO need food, being familiar with local flora and fauna will help. As a general rule of thumb, most furry mammals can be eaten. So can snakes (cut the head off far enough back to remove poison sacs on poisonous species), fish, and insects that aren't furry, brightly colored, or sting. Plants are more of a mixed bag. Some are okay, others will make you sick. Some will kill. It's best to consult a field guide specific to your area for better information. Or use Google. It's quicker.

These steps constitute the most basic of survival tactics. Nothing can replace field experience. If you plan on spending a lot of time in the backcountry, a survival course taught by qualified instructors can be an awesome addition to your knowledge base.

First Aid Kit

In the event you experience any sort of emergency, a first aid kit can literally be a lifesaver. Unfortunately, survival gear takes up a lot of room. Unlike hikers, runners have to be judicious about the gear they carry. What I decide to carry is heavily dependent on local conditions. Trail runs through the relatively safe Michigan countryside aren't nearly as dangerous as backcountry mountain trails. Weather also plays a role. Cold, heat, precipitation, and the availability of shelter factor into the decision of what to carry.

If I'm close to civilization and running on popular, safe trails, I usually don't carry anything. If I'm doing a longer run in a relatively safe environment, I may bring foot care provisions like a few band-aids, alcohol wipes (for sterilization), a safety pin (to lance blisters or remove slivers), and super glue (to close minor wounds).

If I'm running in adverse conditions that could present a danger or I'm traveling farther from civilization, I may carry:

- A butane lighter for firestarting
- A space blanket for makeshift shelters, heat reflector, solar still, cord (if cut in strips), or emergency signaling device
- A small, sharp pocket knife
- A plastic poncho or garbage bag if rain is in the forecast
- A flashlight with fresh batteries
- A few yards of parachute cord
- An emergency whistle

These basic items can be used to build a shelter and build a fire. All these items together take up about as much space and weigh as much as two decks of playing cards and can be carried in a hydration pack, fanny pack (for those who want to channel the 1990s), or water bottle pockets. I've even attached some of that gear to a wide-brimmed straw gardener's hat.

Survival Stuff

Survival skills are great to learn. Unfortunately, a comprehensive explanation of advanced wilderness survival goes beyond the scope of this book. I will, however, share a few of my favorite tips.

In the Cold

Cold weather presents two distinct dangers- losing extremities due to frostbite and dying from hypothermia.

Frostbite occurs when blood stops flowing to a region because of cold-induced vasoconstriction. To prevent frostbite, cover up. A layer of clothing over exposed skin usually prevents frostbite when moving. If you stop, make sure you keep everything covered and as dry as possible. If an area starts to hurt due to cold, warm it slowly. Fingers can be placed against your body. I like armpits. For toes, use a friend's armpits if available. If your face is freezing, bury it in a friend's chest. I use that line on Shelly a lot. If you're alone, build a fire. If you can't build a fire, warm your hands then apply them to the affected area. Repeat as necessary.

Hypothermia is a bigger danger to life. Part of the problem is judgment. When hypothermia begins to set it, people do really stupid stuff like strip off all their clothes. To prevent hypothermia, stay dry and warm moving usually generates enough heat to maintain body temperature, which is the reason we see so few ultrarunning alligators.

You know, they're cold blooded and all.

Anyway, problems usually arise when you're drenched in sweat or fall through ice. If this happens, act immediately. It's usually better to keep clothing on. If you have the capability to build a fire, do so immediately. If not, try to keep moving toward safety. If neither option is available, building shelter may provide a degree of protection from the cold. The wind is usually the killer- if you can effectively block the wind, your chances of survival increase dramatically. If you do build a snow shelter, remember to leave a breathing hole and provide insulation between your body and the snowy walls and floor. If you're with a group, huddle together. The shared body heat can be enough to ward off hypothermia.

In the Heat

Getting too hot presents the same dangers as being too cold, just in the opposite direction. Hyperthermia is a significant danger for runners. Our bodies do a great job of cooling... to a point. In the thermoregulation chapter, I place some of the blame on runners overheating by wearing moisture-wicking clothing in hot, dry weather.

Many ultrarunners erroneously believe that consuming adequate fluids and electrolytes will solve the overheating problem. I call bullshit. If we outpace the body's ability to cool off, we'll develop hyperthermia and could die.

The solution is simple- *stop running when you get too hot.* When you stop moving, you stop generating heat. This process can be aided by seeking shade and dousing your skin or clothing with water. This can be effective because you can use any water source, even if it's polluted. Got a urine fetish? Here's your chance to publicly indulge without fear of social rejection. Who can pass judgment when lives are at stake?

Building a Fire

In the event you're lost or injured, the ability to build a fire could mean the difference between life or death. It can be used for warmth, cooking, signaling, or warding off dangerous animals. Whenever I venture into the backcountry, I always prepare for the possibility of having to build a fire. I've tried several primitive methods of fire-starting. Quite frankly, it's hard. *Really hard.* Instead of pissing with rocks or bows, I carry a simple Bic butane lighter. It is lightweight, reliable, and waterproof. A new lighter could feasibly be used for several weeks of daily fire-starting.

The first step is to find an adequate location for the fire. The purpose of the fire will partially determine location. Ideally, look for a flat, relatively open area free of flammable materials. flat rocks or bare earth are good choices. A dry, grassy field is a not a good choice. Rocks can be used to construct a fire ring which will help contain the fire.

Types of Fires

There are a variety of designs that will serve different purposes. Knowing a few basic designs will increase the efficiency of the fires. Here are the fires I use:

- **Teepee fires:** The fuel for teepee fires is arranged in a pyramid or teepee shape. This fire allows a great deal of oxygen to circulate, producing a hot fire that burns quickly. This is my preferred fire for most occasions, including "let's head out to the wilderness, build a fire, get naked, and drink beer" fires.
- **Log cabin fire:** This fire utilizes horizontal pieces laid in a square alternating from side to side with the initial fire built in the middle. This type of fire doesn't emit as much heat, but lasts longer and provides a flat surface for cooking.
- **Star fire:** A small teepee is built in the middle, then five timbers are placed flat on the ground in the shape of a star. One end is touching the teepee. As the fire burns, the timbers are pushed into the center for fuel. This fire last a long time and can also provide a decent surface for cooking.
- **Trench fire:** This fire is ideal for windy conditions. A 12" by 36" by 12" deep trench is dug running parallel to the prevailing wind. The wind will create a draft to fuel the fire while still providing enough protection to start it. Line the trench with rocks to help radiate heat upward. A fire is built in the middle of the trench. I like to use a teepee design. The trench can also be used to support cookware or skewers.

Starting and Maintaining the Fire

Getting that initial flame is the tough part. The rest is a matter of understanding the basic principles of fire. To build a fire, two things are needed- fuel and oxygen. The fuel can be pretty much anything flammable. Oxygen is obviously present in the air we breathe, but can be enhanced by blowing on flames or building the fire to use wind to provide greater oxygen flow.

First, the fuel issue. When building a fire, start with small flammable materials that have a lot of surface area. This is known as *tinder*. Good tinder could be lint from your belly button, dry pine needles, dry grass, paper, the fluffy fibers from cattails, dry moss, potato chips, nuts, dry leaves, and steel wool. Many runners carry petroleum-based lube or lip balm, both of which can be used to coat tinder to make it burn better. Pine sap can be used in the same way.

Once the kinder is lit, *kindling* can be added. This should be made up of flammable materials slightly larger than the tinder. Small, dry sticks work great. Once they begin to burn, progressively larger timbers can be added as fuel. Some designs, like the log cabin fire, will already have the fuel built into the design. Others, like the teepee, will require fuel to be added. The star design will require the timbers to be pushed toward the center.

Size Matters

The fire should be just large enough to serve the intended purpose. Novices tend to make fires too big, which wastes fuel and increases the danger of igniting the surrounding environment. Start with a small fire, then increase the size as needed. It's easier to increase size than it is to decrease size.

Running with Dogs

As I mentioned earlier, dogs can make an ideal training partner. Here are some tips for those dog-running novices:

- If you're in the market for a dog and your primary goal is to find a running partner, look for a breed that is adept at running. Sled dog breeds, sporting and hunting breeds, and herding dogs all make decent running partners. Toy breeds... not so much.
- Dogs have issues with thermoregulation. They cannot run in hot weather like humans. Humans can cool down while moving due to our sweating mechanism. Dogs will pant to cool down, and will need to stop moving if they overheat. If your dog wants to stop and lie down, it's too hot. Don't continue forcing it to run. If you live in a warm or hot

climate, you will probably have to run early in the morning, late in the evening, or at night.

- Dogs need to work up to longer distances, just like we do. If their first run is a 20 miler, odds are good they'll get hurt.
- Get a good leash. Avoid retractable leashes.
- Take time training the dog. Before taking your dog out on the trails, it should be able to reliably come when called, sit, stay, and be able to run at your side without excessive pulling.

Running Naked

Okay, this isn't so much a trail running tip as a personal challenge. Trail running is a very cool experience. It's even better nude. We live in an overly prudish society that implicitly (or explicitly) teaches us to be ashamed of our bodies. Imagine how much our society would improve if everyone recognized their own inner beauty?

It's easy enough to do. All you need is either a remote trail or the cover of darkness. Make sure you're either in an area that's nudity-friendly (i.e., you won't be arrested), on private property, or are a long, long way from civilization. Strip down; run around. If you love the feeling of freedom, you'll love the experience!

Not ready for that sort of commitment? Start with some occasional flashing. Better yet, try a naked race. There are several naked 5k races held throughout the U.S.

Ultramarathons!

Why You Should Run Ultras

Prize money?

No. Even if you win, you probably can't even pay for the food you ate during the race.

Fame?

Nope. People will think you're crazy... and not "the party doesn't start until you arrive" kind of crazy.

Health?

Not even close. I usually feel about twenty years older after finishing a race.

So why bother? It comes down to one simple fact- you'll never be this young again. There's nothing more empowering than completing a race 99.99% of the human population would never even consider, let alone attempt. You'll forever compare an ultra finish to difficult life events. You'll realize you really can accomplish far more than you expect. This empowering experience can be life-changing.

Since Shelly and I adopted our hobo lifestyle (we live in an RV and travel frequently), we've come across a few tough times. The experience of running hundos has reinforced the idea that I can survive pretty much anything as long as I keep moving forward.

There may be other reasons, too. You get cool swag, like shirts, belt buckles, and beer mugs. You get to experience nature up close and personal. You get to brag to your friends. You can say douchy stuff like "You run marathons? Awwww... how cute!" You meet incredible people and bond over your mutual struggles. You get to poop in the woods. And the groupies... can't forget the groupies!

Okay, there are no groupies. In fact, the only people that seem to be attracted to sweaty, smelly ultrarunners are, well, other ultrarunners.

Still not convinced? Start hanging out with ultrarunners. Volunteer to work at an aid station for a local race. Google "ultramarathon race report", then read a few. Crew or pace a friend as they complete an ultra. I guarantee you'll catch the bug!

What does it take to Run Ultras?

So you're still deciding if you want to tackle the ultramarathon distance. You're intrigued by the idea, but you have doubts. What exactly does it take to run ultras? As it turns out, it's probably not as difficult as one would imagine.

First, it does take some degree of physical fitness. If your goal is to simply finish the race, it is critical that you have the ability to spend a long period of time on your feet. The "time on feet" will likely be a combination of running and walking. How will you know you are ready? I like to use a 50% guideline. If you can estimate your finish time in the planned ultra, your training should allow you to spend at least 50% of that time on a single long run. For example, let's say you are planning a 50 mile run. You anticipate finishing in 10 hours. You could probably survive the distance if you are able to do a training run of at least five hours. Greater fitness will obviously increase the chances of finishing, but the 50% guideline is useful to determine minimal readiness.

Second, completing an ultra takes training. I do have a good friend, Rich Elliott, that attempted a 50 mile race with a single 5k as his only training. He made it to about 27 miles before he DNFed (did not finish.) That was foolish. Brave, but foolish. In my opinion, one can get by with only a few runs per week and still finish an ultra as long as one of the runs is a long run of ever-increasing distance. Since the guide is for the lazy runners like me, I can admit to rarely running more than three or four days per week.

Third, ultrarunners need to be reasonably familiar with the issues they may face when running very long distances. They must be aware of the signs and symptoms of problems and know the appropriate response. In marathon-and-shorter races, most runners can simply run. If an issue arises, you can gut it out to the finish. In an ultra, that is usually impossible. It's awfully hard to gut out a chafed groin for eight hours.

Fourth, ultrarunners need to be mentally tough. You will experience some degree of pain. In all likelihood, you will experience A LOT of pain. In my first 100 mile attempt that ultimately resulted in a DNF at mile 65, I seriously considered diving on rocks to break an arm just to end the suffering of having to continue. Luckily I was too scared... instead I just let the cutoff times catch me and was mercifully pulled from the course. My problem was simple- I hadn't developed very good strategies for dealing with the pain. The second attempt hurt a lot, too, but I practiced much better pain-management strategies.

These are what I would consider to be the absolute minimum elements to running an ultra. Other things like prior racing experience, outdoor survival skills, an uncanny ability to navigate through the wilderness, being especially athletically gifted, or single with no children will certainly help. They are not necessities, though. Almost everyone has the ability to run ultras... even those that may not believe it today. If you can reasonably master these four elements, you will be in an excellent position to conquer the ultramarathon distances!

Don't you have to be a Good Runner?

There's a myth that runners have to be good to run ultramarathons. By "good" I mean fast. Sure, many ultrarunners are blazing fast in shorter races. It's not a prerequisite, though. It's entirely possible to be turtle-slow and still finish an ultra. I would go out on a limb and say it may be advantageous to be slow.

Generally speaking, there's an inverse relationship between speed and distance. As distances increase speed (as measured by pace) decreases. Once you get to ultra distances, the non-elites are pretty slow. How slow? When I finished my first 100, my average pace was around 17:30. No, that's not a typo. Yes, most people can walk faster than that. The point... it's a VERY slow average pace. Even at my fastest, I doubt I ran more than 10 minute miles.

In ultras, slow is the name of the game. If you already run slow... perfect! You won't have to learn how to restrain yourself in the early miles of ultras. Many novice runners start out way too fast, which results in a severe crash-and-burn. The ability to run slow is an under-appreciated skill set.

I know you're still doubting me. You've convinced yourself that speed is a necessary ingredient to building long distance running ability. Unfortunately this belief keeps many runners from ever attempting an ultra. They convince themselves that they have to reach some arbitrary time-based goal at a shorter distance before they can make the jump to ultras. I know people that can run 100+ miles per week, easily drop Boston-qualifying times in marathons, and can recite the ingredients and nutritional value of every energy gel, bar, and drink on the market. Yet they doubt their ability to survive an ultra.

If your goal is to simply finish (and it should be if this is your first ultra AND you are truly a lazy runner), pick a goal race... maybe a 50k. Find out the cutoff time (how long you are allowed to finish before everyone packs up and goes home.) Go to the cool running pace calculator here: http://www.coolrunning.com/engine/4/4_1/96.shtml. Enter the cutoff time and the distance; it will return your pace. Now go out and run a few miles at that pace.

-STOP AND GO RUN-

Okay, now that you're back, how was that pace? Pretty slow, huh? I bet it felt like you weren't even moving. I bet your normal training pace doesn't feel too slow now. That is the minimum you would need to finish the race. Anyone can do that. Don't worry, I'll give you more advice in the coming days... just have confidence that your slow running is an asset in ultras!

The Different Race Options

The first step to choosing that first ultra is actually choosing the race. The single best resource is Ultrarunning Magazine's online ultra calendar (http://www.ultrarunning.com/calendar.html). The races can be sorted in a variety of ways based on location, distance, difficulty, date, etc. I would recommend starting with distance. There are actually two categories: distance races and timed races. Here are the most common:

- **50k (31 miles):** This is considered the minimum "ultra" distance. It's usually considered to be the easiest. It's a good first choice, especially if you don't want to train for a long period of time.
- **50 miles:** This is also a decent choice for a first ultra. It's more difficult, but can still be run in a single day.
- **100k:** This distance is getting into the realm of "too difficult for a first ultra" because it usually requires day and night running.
- **100 miles:** Some people start with hundos, but I'd advise against it. You encounter a lot of issues that are difficult to experience in training. Your best bet is to learn from the shorter distances first.
- **6 hour race:** This is probably the shortest timed race where a beginner could reach the ultra distance (50k). The races are usually held on short looped courses with ample aid and other support. However, it would probably require running for the entire 6 hours, and averaging about an 11:30 minute/mile pace. It is probably better to do a...
- **12 hour race:** This is a great ultra distance to get your feet wet if a 50k distance race is unavailable. Pretty much anybody can reach the ultra distance and still have plenty of time to sit down and rest, eat, and take care of any issues that arise. Think of it as an ultra with training wheels for the newbie. In fact, 12 hours are my favorite race to introduce people to ultra distances. I use using simple logic: you can stop at any time, even after one lap.
- **24 hour race:** This is another good option if a 12 hour race isn't available. It can also be a good option for those wanting to train for 100 milers since it involves night running and sleep deprivation.
- **48 and 72 hour races:** This would be overkill for a newbie... no need to go this long unless you're really into adventure!

As if this wasn't enough options, races also come in a few different layouts:

- **Point-to-point:** This race starts at one place and ends at another. Timed races do not use this format. Personally this is my favorite type of race because you don't run on the same part of the course twice. I like the novelty. For beginners, this is a good choice because you don't come back to the start line, which could give you the opportunity to drop out of the race (DNF, or Did Not Finish).
- **Loop:** A looped course is run in a series of, well, loops. All timed races are loop races. Many distance races run in smaller parks are also looped course. The advantage of loops is course familiarity. Once you run one loop, you've seen all of the course. For some, this is a nice benefit. If

you have masochistic friends and family that want to watch you run for the better part of a day, looped courses are ideal.

- **Out-and-back:** These races start at one point, run to another, then back to the original start line. They have the advantage of course familiarity on the way back, but also make it difficult to stop. Unless you have a rise to the start line, dropping out would still require you to walk all the way back to the start line- the same distance you'd cover if you stayed in the race. Personally, I like to plan training runs as out-and-backs for this very reason.
- **Stage Races:** These races are held over the course of a few days. You run a certain distance, rest, then run more the next day. Because of the logistics, these really aren't good "newbie" races... and some question if it is actually an ultramarathon if the runners don't cover at least 50k per day.

Choosing Your First Ultramarathon

If you ask experienced ultrarunners, they will often recommend a specific race as an "ideal first race." Here's the problem- it's the race they recommend *based on their experiences*. Sometimes they're right. Sometimes they're wrong. Their suggestions certainly deserve consideration, but I'd recommend tailoring the choice a little more based on this criteria:

1. Choose a distance that you can realistically train for given the time frame. If you're choosing a 50k, a few months will probably be sufficient. A 50 miler will take more time, as will a 100k or a 100 miler. You have more latitude with timed races since you can run whatever distance you want.

2. Pick a race that features terrain and elevation similar to your training grounds. If you live in Florida where hills are non-existent, it's probably a bad idea to sign up for a mountain ultra with thousands of feet of climbing and descending. It's the same deal with terrain. Don't sign up for a notoriously rocky ultra if you routinely get passed by soccer moms pushing jogging strollers on your local trails. The Ultrarunning Magazine online calendar has a handy 1-5 rating scale for both terrain and elevation with the higher number representing more elevation and more technical trails.

3. Bring experienced friends. Nothing can be more valuable than the support of friends that have ultra experience. When I ran my first ultra, I was helped by a dude that had run several hundred ultras in his lifetime. He ran with me for about 12 miles and kept me from quitting when I hit some serious lows. Since relying on strangers can be difficult, set the stage by asking a friend to run the race side by side with you. If you can't find a willing or experienced friend, join some online ultrarunning communities. It's usually pretty easy to make friends, then ask them for the same favor. If it helps, offer to pay their entry fee.

4. Don't bite off more than you can chew. The longer the distance, the more likely issues will arise that will have to be solved. For example, 100 milers require you to navigate trails in the dark while both fatigued and sleep-deprived. It's difficult to get the needed experience in training. The fewer the variables, the greater your chances of success. You'll have plenty of opportunities to tackle the toughies down the road.

Considering these three issues can go a long way toward finding your "ideal" first ultra. The goal is to put you in a position to succeed, and then use that success to conquer greater challenges in the future.

Learning about the Race

Now that you've signed up (and nursed that hangover), you can start researching the intricate details of the race. You'll want to know important things like:

- The race rules
- Lodging options in the area
- Typical weather conditions
- How other runners approached the race

All of these items can be found on the race websites or by reading race reports. When some people run a race, they write race reports to document their experience. These can be found in a number of places, including ultrarunning forums, blogs, or ultrarunning websites. Some race directors even post race reports on the race website. An easy way to find them is Googling "[insert race name] race report."

Don't discount the best possible resource- runners who have first-hand knowledge of the course or race. If the race is local, it should be pretty easy to find runners who have run the race. Check with local running clubs or running stores.

Elevation Profiles

In the last section I mentioned elevation. Most race directors publish what is known as an elevation profile. It's essentially a graph representing how many hills the course has. The "spikier" the graph, the more hills. Also, the steeper the graph, the steeper the hill.

Many recommend a flat course for beginners. Again, I'd recommend picking a course with similar climbs and altitude as your training trails. People who train in the rough stuff usually have some difficulty going to the flat stuff.

If you train at high altitude, you can run a race at lower altitude without problems. Going from low-altitude training to a high altitude (> 8,000 feet) race can be problematic, though. The lower concentration of oxygen can cause altitude sickness. Unless that's your thing. Sure it can be life-threatening, but some people may be into nosebleeds, hangover symptoms, and cerebral edema. To each their own... I guess.

How Much Do Ultramarathons Cost?

The price of ultras can range from free (fatass races) to staggeringly expensive. Badwater, a race run through Death Valley in California, can easily cost around $10,000 for the race entry fee, hotels, gear, and rental vehicles. So what is a more realistic price?

Most races range in price from a low of about $30 to a high of about $300. Generally speaking, the longer the race, the more expensive the entry fees. Other variables make a difference, like the level of support offered, the need for permits to use the land, and the swag (goodies like t-shirts and finisher awards).

Aside from the entry fee, other costs need to be considered, including:

- **Transportation**: If the race is within driving distance, you need to consider the price of gas and parking. If the race requires flying, consider airport parking, the cost of the flight, rental car, and gas.
- **Lodging**: Hotels may be needed for the night before and after the race. Hint- always get a room on the first floor. After the race, it will likely be difficult to climb stairs. Some races will offer on-site camping, which can save money. If you camp in a tent, bring plenty of warm blankets. It's not uncommon to feel colder than normal after a race.
- **Food**: You will need food before and after the race, and potentially food during the race. Some races offer pre- and post-race meals. One of the best parts of ultrarunning is that we tend to burn a lot of calories, which means one thing: guilt-free fast food! I recommend Taco Bell. Lay off the spicy sauces, though... otherwise you'll regret it the next day. Trust me on this one.
- **Gear**: I prefer to bring as little gear as possible, but it still adds up to a fair amount of crap. I usually bring several clothing options, at least two pair of shoes, sometimes socks (I hate socks), bandana, flashlights and headlamps, lube (prevent chafing), handheld water bottles, and a small foot care kit (I'll discuss that one later). For very long races, I'll also add some more crap to my stockpile. To save money, you can often use non-running specific 'homemade" gear. In my first ultra, I used little travel bottles designed for shampoo ($1 each) instead of gel

flasks designed for runners ($12 each). Different sections of this book will help you determine what you need to buy.

There may be other expenses that arise based on individual experiences. For the most part, ultras are pretty cheap compared to other hobbies. The closer you stay to home, the more money you'll likely save on transportation and lodging.

What About Fatass Races?

Is this a race for people with giant butts? Not quite. A fatass race is essentially an organized "unofficial" race set up by one or a few dedicated ultrarunners. There are no perks (shorts, medals, etc.), course marshals (people who keep you on the course), aid stations or other forms of support, or even a timing mechanism. It's usually more like a training run than a race.

So why would you want to run a fatass?

THEY'RE FREE!

And they tend to be super cool. The people who show up for fatass races are running for the pure love of running and the camaraderie of their fellow runners. I would highly encourage any new ultrarunner to hang out at fatass races.

However, I would not recommend a fatass as a first race. The lack of support usually requires runners to carry all their food and water, which adds a fairly difficult obstacle to an already big undertaking. Also, the lack of course markings may make the actual course navigation difficult. Again, it's another variable that a brand new ultrarunner shouldn't have to worry about.

The Difference between Road and Trail Ultras

The vast majority of ultras are run on trails of some sort. Some are run on roads. Distance races tend to be more trail-oriented, while timed races tend to be more road-oriented (which may include things like running tracks or concrete sidewalks through parks).

Is one better than the other?

Not necessarily, though there are significant differences. Road running requires a lot of repetitive motions. Your running gait remains more or less the same for the duration of the event. Furthermore, road races tend to be rather flat. This puts stress on specific sets of muscles, tendons, ligaments, and bones. People like me who train primarily on trails usually have difficulty running on roads.

Most trail runs require the runner to avoid obstacles such as roots, rocks, logs (both wooden and the kind left by animals... or lazy humans), and water or mud. Trail races tend to have more elevation change, so you spend more time traversing hills. This requires much more dynamic movement, which distributes the workload to different muscles, tendons, ligaments, and bones. People that train primarily on roads usually have difficulty running on trails.

My suggestion: It's best to choose a race with similar terrain and elevation as your training routes. If you live in a city surrounded by flat farmland, a mountain trail race would be a bad idea. It's the same deal if you like to train on trails with lots of elevation change. A road race will be more difficult than a trail race.

It is possible to take a "jack of all trades" approach and train on both roads and trails, which gives you MUCH more versatility. This would be the ideal situation if you have enough time to train before your first ultra.

Taking the Leap and Signing Up

Okay, so you found the perfect race. Now what? I bet you're a little hesitant to register. I have a time-tested method to alleviate that uneasy feeling when you're filling out the registration form. Here's what you need:

- A computer (or mail-in form, envelope, and stamp for those races that are still stuck in the 1900s)
- Credit card (or check book)
- A good friend or relative with an antagonistic personality
- Copious amounts of your favorite alcohol

Step One: Explain the antagonist's role- to get you to sign up for the race.
Step Two: Go to race website registration page.
Step Three: Drink all of the alcohol.
Step Four: Let the antagonist work their magic.

Congratulations! You just signed up for your first ultra!

Now tell everyone you know. The more people you tell, the more social pressure you'll feel to follow through and not back out at the last minute.

Enter social networks.

Nothing makes a better Facebook post than "I just signed up for my first 50 miler!"

Finding the Time to Train for Ultras

Ultramarathons must take a ton of training. Don't they?

That's a question I receive more than any other. Well, aside from "Why do you do it?" People are hesitant to make the plunge into the world of ultras because the training appears so intimidating. It must take a gargantuan weekly time commitment to prepare your body to run 31+ miles at one time.

Yes and no.

It is possible to run an ultra on very little training. Rich Elliott, a good friend, decided to run a 50 miler with no training. His lone training run consisted of a 5k a few weeks prior. That's it. He ran 3.1 miles in two years. On race day, he managed to eek out 27 miles before throwing in the towel.

John DeVries, another good friend, ran a 12 hour timed ultra with a single 8 mile run in the previous two years. He made it to about 22 miles. Off topic, but check out John's adventures as he travels the Americas on his motorcycle: http://motovagabond.net/

What can be learned from their experiences? It's tough to run an ultra with no training. If you have a little bit of a running background, you could probably do it with minimal training. If you have a strong running background, you can probably do it with the training you already have.

The correlation should be obvious- the more you train, the better the results. I would go a step further and say the more you train, the *more enjoyable the race will be.*

It does take time. This *is* a huge undertaking, and you *will* have work to do it. There are no substitutes or shortcuts- you have to put in the hours. It's not like triathlons where you can drop a grand on aerodynamic berets or fancy "lighter-than-farts" bolts to save a few ounces... you gotta bust your ass!

However, these hours don't have to be intimidating. You don't have to add a ton of training hours on top of your already busy schedule. The trick is to merge your ultra training with your existing daily life.

Not only is it possible, it's the norm. Ultrarunning is a unique sport. Even the best of the best don't make enough money from sponsorships or race winnings to make a living. In fact, this money rarely pays for the races themselves. Pretty much all ultrarunners have normal jobs. They have to figure out how to fit ultrarunning into their lives.

The secret is deceptively simple:

Always train.

No, I don't mean skirt all your responsibilities, sell the kids on eBay, and start running ten hours each day. Look at everything you do on a daily basis and begin asking:

How can I tweak this activity to achieve some training benefit?

Turn everything in your life into an opportunity to train. By simply re-framing the situation, you don't have to worry about carving four hours each day from your already busy life. Instead you are now free to train 24 hours a day, seven days a week! Day at the office? Training. Picking up toilet bowl cleaner from the grocery store? Training. Puttin' the moves on your significant other? Training. Yes, you read that right. Sounds more fun than running around a track, huh?

I know what some of you are thinking: but I don't have a significant other! Worry not strong-armed friends, I have at least one tip for you, too.

Most of the advice I give in this book revolves around this idea- you can train pretty much everywhere, no matter what you're doing.

Balancing Life Commitments

Training for ultras takes significant time, even if you go to great lengths to incorporate training in every element of your daily life. Managing your family and/or professional life can be a challenge. If you don't have a spouse, kids, or even a job, ride that wave as long as you can. You'll never have this much free time again. Well, at least not for a number of decades.

In the event you do have a spouse, kids, and/or a career, balancing these responsibilities can be a challenge. Here's some practical advice:

- **Set priorities.** Mine always went something like this: Time with spouse, time with kids, ultra training, catching up on my favorite TV shows, work-related stuff, chores, grooming facial hair.
- **Develop a training schedule that has a minimal impact on other responsibilities.** This may involve training after everyone else goes to bed or before they wake up in the morning.
- **If you have to miss a workout, don't fret.** Missing a single workout isn't going to doom your plan.
- **Give your spouse plenty of time to follow their own hobbies.** We all need our own "me" time. It may also help to lavish them with gifts.
- **Understand that most opposition to an ultrarunning spouse is rooted in resentment.** The non-running spouse feels as if they are shouldering an unfair burden. Having open, honest communication about sharing responsibilities will usually cure this issue.
- **Bring your kids with you using a jogging stroller or, if they're old enough, have them ride their bike behind you.** Better yet, have them man an aid station for you.
- **Get your spouse hooked on running ultras, too.** It's better to fight over who gets to train than having to defend the need to train. And the endorphines will probably enhance your sex life. Win-win.

When I was building my endurance base early in my ultrarunning days, Shelly and I were having lots of babies. When the babies got on a fairly reliable sleep schedule, I'd leave to run after they woke up in the middle of the night. I would tend to their needs, then put them back to sleep. Once they were sleeping, I'd run. This allowed Shelly to sleep for a few hours undisturbed and allowed me to stick to my training plan. As our kids aged, finding time to train became easier.

Is There Such Thing as a Perfect Career for Ultramarathoners?

When I talked about the idea of thinking of every moment of your life as an opportunity to train, I bet you started considering your profession. I did the same thing. I used to be a high school teacher. When I started running ultras, I looked for every opportunity I could find to train.

It started with parking as far away from the front doors as possible, which forced me to walk farther. If I had to go anywhere around the school and time wasn't an issue, I took a route that would bring me up and down multiple sets of stairs. Sometimes I would eat a huge lunch, sometimes I would fast (I'll explain later). When teaching, I'd stand on a balance board to build balance and core strength. I would even do some air squats and walking lunges at the beginning and end of every day to help develop leg strength.

There are some careers that can offer even more opportunities to train. Anyone who spends time on their feet can think of that as a form of training. Lift heavy objects? That builds strength. Work in a skyscraper? What better way to develop hill climbing and descending ability than avoiding the elevator. Exotic dancer? Pole dancing is perhaps the best core-building exercise out there.

If you are interested in ultras and happen to be looking for a career, consider the training prospects. Something like a walking mail delivery route could make for wonderful training. Better yet, how about working as a mountain guide? Working in an office? Look for a place that will allow a stand-up desk. Better yet, how about a treadmill desk?

If you're not fortunate enough to be in the market for a new career, look at your present career. Make a game out of finding training opportunities. This book will give you lots of ideas. It's up to you to retrofit them to your occupation.

Ben VanHoose and Jeremiah Cataldo

Give Me a Training Plan!

Here are a few popular training plans for the new ultrarunner. This isn't meant to be an exhaustive list, but a few examples to give you a taste of what's out there. I've used a few and will give my own comments when appropriate.

- **Crossfit/ Crossfit Endurance**: Crossfit is a functional fitness-based workout program designed to develop multiple areas of athletic skills. CF *Endurance* adds an element of high-intensity anaerobic running to the mix. The theory goes something like this: By running long, slow distances, we get slower and weaker. If we do shorter distance high intensity running combined with functional fitness training, we get faster and stronger at running (and any other athletic endeavor). I've used CF/CFE in the past, and still use many elements of the program. It's good. However, the lack of long runs severely dampens the ability to experiment with all of the variables inherent in ultras (like gear,

90

food, chafing, etc.) If you like your workouts to end with lying in the fetal position in a pool of your own vomit, this is the plan for you.

- **Maffetone Method**: The Maffetone Method pretty much takes the opposite approach. It replaces all high-intensity workouts with long, slow runs. The Maffetone method uses a heart rate monitor to keep heart rate below a predetermined point to train your body to utilize fat burning. Higher intensity workouts can be added after an endurance base has been built. I have played around with the Maffetone heart rate monitoring, and it does work as advertised. If you don't like sweating, this is the plan for you.

- **Modified Hal Higdon plan**: Hal Higdon's marathon training programs have been guiding marathoners to the finish line for... well, forever. His plans have a balance of different types of runs based on experience. The tricky part- his plans are designed for marathons. They can be modified easily, though. If you like doing what everybody else is doing, this is the plan for you.

- **Jeff Galloway-based plan**: Galloway's plans, like Higdon's, are designed for marathons. However, Galloway's plan differs by utilizing a system of running and walking intervals. This concept is one of the most popular techniques used in ultras. As such, his training plan is quite popular. So popular in fact, ultrarunner Tim Looney refers to ultras as giant "Gallo-walking festivals." If you spend your mornings doing laps at the local mall and watched 'The Golden Girls' because of all the hotties, this is the plan for you.

- **Runner's World plan**: Runners World produced an ultra training plan, but it assumes you've already run a marathon. Still, some people like Runner's World. Their forums are pretty cool. And some people like the incredible diversity of their magazine's cover art. You know, a skinny white girl with ash blonde hair one month, then a skinny white girl with strawberry blonde hair the next. Anyway, here's the plan: http://www.runnersworld.com/article/0,7120,s6-238-244--7556-0,00.html

- **Santa Clara Runners customizable plan**: This plan is really cool- it's an interactive website that produces a customized plan. The plan itself is basic; there are no specifications for different types of runs. Still, it will get you to the finish line. Check it out here: http://www.scrunners org/ultrasch.php

- **The plan from *The Barefoot Running Book***: I wrote a plan included in my other book, but it's designed for marathons. Same deal as Higdon and Galloway's plans... it can be modified for ultras. It's really a hybrid that combines Crossfit and Crossfit-style workouts designed in conjunction with my friend Pete Kemme of Kemme Fitness (http://kemmefitness.com) and Maffetone's long, slow runs. It's the best of both worlds. Now run out and buy the book. :-)

- *Relentless Forward Progress* **plan**: Bryon Powell's excellent book *'Relentless Forward Progress'* includes an excellent plan based on Bryon's own experiences. Bryon is the editor-in-chief of_irunfar.com, THE ultramarathon resource on the 'web. If you're looking for a more legitimate, serious book by ultrarunners that are actually *talented, hard-working runners*, check out his book.

Check out each of these. Using the criteria I shared earlier, pick the plan that will be a good fit for you. If you can't decide, pick the plan from The Barefoot Running Book. If you are offended by my shameless cross-promotion, pick Crossfit. Then send me the pictures of you lying in that pool of vomit.

How Do You Choose a Training Plan?

Okay, let's get down to the nitty-gritty of ultra training- the plan. The training plan is the backbone of your quest to finish your first ultra. If you do a quick Internet search, you'll find dozens of plans dedicated specifically to ultras. On top of that, you'll also find hundreds of marathon training plans that feasibly could be modified for ultras.

You probably want me to recommend one specific plan, huh?

Too bad. I'm going to make YOU choose. I'll give you some guidance, but ultimately the decision has to be yours to make.

I presented a few of the more popular plans above. The following is the criteria I recommend to make the choice. You should be able to quickly peruse the details of each plan and get an idea of those which might work well for you.

Let's start with the criteria. These should be your primary considerations:

- **Consideration #1: What distance am I running?** Some plans are specifically tailored to a given distance. Others can be modified for any distance. You can start by eliminating those which cannot be modified to fit your given distance.

92

- **Consideration #2: How does the schedule of training runs (and crosstraining in some cases) fit your life?** If you work 80 hours a week, a plan that requires several long, slow runs each week probably won't work. Make sure the plan fits your time allotment. And stop pissing away your life by working too much.
- **Consideration #3: Does this running plan have a community I can lean on for support?** Some plans (like Crossfit Endurance) have an active community of people going through the exact same thing you are. It can be handy to lean on them for support and guidance as you progress toward the race.

Using Heart Rate as a Training Tool

If you chose the Maffetone Method in the "Give Me a Training Plan!" section, you'll become intimately familiar with heart rate monitors. Even if you didn't, a heart rate monitor could be a valuable tool. Not only is it cool to see your heart rate in real time, it can be used as a great training tool to prepare your body for ultras.

The idea goes something like this: If you run slow enough, your body will burn primarily fat instead of carbohydrates. Since most of us have well over 100,000 "fat" calories stored in our body and only a few thousand "carb" calories, it makes sense to burn the fat. Besides that, the "bonk" or "wall" marathoners complain about is caused by your bodily supply of carbohydrates running low.

It's actually really easy to train your body to burn fat. I do two things:

First, run your long runs slow. This is where a heart rate monitor comes into play. If you keep your heart rate low (here's Maffetone's formula: http://philmaffetone.com/180formula.cfm) on your long runs, you'll train your body to better utilize fat stores. There are other possible positive benefits, but this is a biggie.

Second, do at least a few of your runs after fasting. Don't eat for 12-24 hours prior to the run. You will reach the "wall" much faster as your body's supply of carbohydrates will be much lower. This isn't nearly as effective as the first technique, but it does familiarize you to the feelings associated with hitting that wall. If you experience the beginnings of those same feelings in a race, eating something sugary will usually reverse the effects. Knowing your body and the signals it's sending is important.

Do You Have to Follow the Plan Religiously?

Now that you have a plan, the next question revolves around adaptability. Do you have to follow the plan precisely?

It probably depends on who you ask.

Those with a type "A" personality will insist you follow the workout precisely. If you miss a run, the world will come crashing down. It's a moot point, though, because your run should be at the top of your list of the other 498 things you have to do each day.

As you probably guessed, I'm not really a list-making kind of person. I'm more of a realist. I'm also guessing you're not really a type "A" personality, either. After all, you *are* reading a book of questionable quality with a ridiculous title written by a mediocre runner.

If you miss a run, it's not a big deal. In fact, taking a break occasionally gives your body time to heal. If you DO miss a workout, just move on to the next one.

Listening to Your Body

In the barefoot running world, we CONSTANTLY talk about the idea of listening to your body. This is a more palatable way of saying "*If it hurts, stop or do something else.*"

The same concept applies to ultrarunning. If you're doing something that causes pain, you're probably doing it wrong. Learn to listen to the signals your body gives, and then adjust accordingly.

Of course, there's a serious problem with this advice. Running really long distances hurts. A lot. Veteran ultrarunners usually refer to it as "discomfort", not "pain." Don't be fooled, *it's fucking pain.*

94

I'll give you some tips to deal with the pain later on, but it does leave us with the question- how do you know if it's *"I'm injured"* pain or *"This is just normal pain everybody experiences when running ultras"*?

The question is difficult to answer. Experience will teach you the difference. But what do you do in the interim? Follow these tips:

Here's my annoying disclaimer: I'm not a medical professional, and I'd recommend consulting one before doing any of this.

1. Generally speaking, muscle soreness is okay. If you've ever lifted weights, it's that feeling you have when you first started. Never felt that? Here's a demo. Do 100 pushups as quickly as possible. Pause to rest if needed, but the quicker the better. That burning you feel? That's usually okay. Stop reading and come back tomorrow.

[one day later]

Feel that soreness in your pecs? That pain is okay, too.

2. Sharp shooting pains are generally bad. If it feels like someone is impaling you with a burning hot fireplace poker, you should stop. Rest until the pain subsides, seek medical attention if needed.

3. If you experience dull aches hours or a day after a workout, that could be bad. Rest until the pain subsides, seek medical attention if needed.

4. Some types of pain are bad. If you experience any weird sensations or symptoms like discoloration, pain that isn't muscular, chest pain, light-headedness, abnormal swelling, fever, weight gain, or anything else abnormal, *seek immediate medical attention.* Always better to be safe than sorry. And there's always a chance the ambulance driver/nurse/doctor will be hot.

Overtraining

Rest days are important. So much so, I'm placing this section ahead of the actually training ideas. When you decide to run an ultra, there's usually some degree of panic that sets in. It's not uncommon to have a

"OH MY GOD, I'M NOT GOING TO BE READY FOR THIS!" feeling. That sometimes drives us to train again and again without giving our body time to recover.

Most of the plans have build-in rest days. TAKE THEM! Your body needs that time to recover.

If you don't rest, there's a chance you will develop overtraining symptoms, which include:

- A higher-than-normal heart rate, which can be measured when waking up in the morning (before those eight cups of coffee)
- Constant muscle soreness
- Insomnia
- Depression-like symptoms
- Loss of appetite
- Loss of motivation
- Irritability

The tricky part of diagnosing overtaining is the symptoms are hard to distinguish from other negative life events, like your favorite reality TV show being canceled or your pet gerbil dying.

I've encountered overtraining occasionally. My challenge has been deciphering the symptoms of overtraining from my natural procrastination and laziness. Lack of motivation? Check. Irritability? If I'm trying to kick that eight cup-a-day coffee habit: check. Insomnia? If there's a SpongeBob marathon on Nickelodeon: check.

For me the tell-tale sign is loss of appetite. It never happens. I once ate an entire large pepperoni pizza in the middle of a bout of the stomach flu. It wasn't pretty.

If you start experiencing overtraining symptoms, what's the best solution? Take a one week vacation. No matter where you are in training, take a week off. Do nothing. The effects on training will be minimal and you'll come back stronger than ever.

Training Partners

Before we get to the nuts and bolts of experimentation ideas, let's chat about training partners. Some people are attracted to ultras for the solitude when training. Or, as was my case, you're looking for a little peace and quiet from your screaming newborn. If this is you, there's no need for a training partner or partners... enjoy the silence.

For those of you that prefer a more social setting, finding good training partners can be invaluable. I have the benefit of having an ultrarunning spouse. In fact, many of the "dates" Shelly and I go on involve running up and down mountains. We also have a great network of friends collectively known as the "Hobby Joggas." We routinely go on group runs then hit up a local bar afterward.

Here are some tips to find training partners:

Tip #1: Find other ultrarunners. Social networking is great for this. Facebook is teeming with runners, many probably live near you. Connecting with them is easy, and most are always looking for new training partners. It's also a great way to get advice from those that have more experience.

Tip #2: Convince your friends to join you on this adventure. If your friends are adventurous, they'll probably join with little hesitation. If they are not adventurous, just lie by omission. If you're training for a 50k, tell them you're training for a 5k and just start going through the training plan. At some point they will catch on. At that point, just say "Oh, did I say *5k*, I meant *50k*! I've always had trouble with zeros."

Tip #3: Get a dog that likes to run. They make great training partners. I'd suggest some sort of sled dog breed. I used to own a Pomeranian, which is apparently a descendant of sled dogs. Once trained, he could easily run 20+ miles as long as the temperatures were cool. Other active breeds will work, too. Avoid dogs like bulldogs as they aren't well-suited for running. Avoid little dogs like miniature pinschers, wiener dogs, or Chihuahuas, too. That just looks silly.

Training Run Conversations

Now that you have a training partner, you may need some help with conversation topics. Well, if you have social skills like me, you could use some help. The rest of you socially-competent folks are fine. Go ahead and skip this section.

Those long runs can last forever, so these should help fill the awkward lulls. I'm dividing the topics based on familiarity with the training partner.

Partner you just met:

- Weather
- Movies you've recently watched
- Running history, how and why you started
- Profession
- Kids (if you have them... otherwise pets are acceptable)

Someone you've known for a few weeks:

- Educational history
- Family history
- Food preferences/diet
- Observations about other runners you see on the trail, but stay positive
- Favorite childhood cartoons and/or toys

Someone you've been running with for months:

- Political views
- Religious views
- Philosophy of life
- Dreams and aspirations
- Whether you sleep in the nude or prefer pajamas
- Annoying co-workers

Someone you've been running with for at least a year:

- Details of the poop you just took in the woods (color, consistency, etc.)
- How different sports bras and/or shorts keep your breasts or genitals from bouncing
- Your real dreams and aspirations that you were too embarrassed to admit earlier
- Your top five erogenous zones
- Best place to dispose of the bodies of those annoying coworkers
- That trip to Cancun, the video on the internet, and your resulting illegitimate child

How to Get Rid of that Annoying Training Partner

I've been lucky- all of my training partners have been great. However, I do occasionally get questions about annoying training partners. Specifically, how do you gracefully get rid of them. Here are some approaches:

Method One: Be direct. Simply tell them "I don't want to run with you anymore. You annoy the shit out of me." If you want to make it more dramatic, add something like "Remember on our last run when you talked nonstop for six hours about how barefoot running changed your life? I spent the entire time contemplating the pros and cons of murder versus suicide." This is probably the healthiest approach and the only one I'd recommend. Maybe skip that last part.

Method Two: Be passive aggressive. This rarely works and is totally unhealthy, but some people find it fun. Or it's a manifestation of a fucked up childhood. Start by showing up 15 minutes late to every run. Next, escalate it by having them run first on trails through wooded areas so they hit all the spider webs spanning across the trail. When running side-by-side, most of us like to run on one side or the other. Figure out their preference then always run on the *opposite* side. If they duck off the trail to relieve themselves, tell them you'll be the lookout. Look the other way when another runner approaches so they're caught in a compromising position. Finally, invite them to a Mexican restaurant the night before a long run. Insist on ordering a bean-heavy dish. The next day, mix up the anti-diarrhea medication with a laxative, tell them you'll bring the toilet paper on the run, and then conveniently forget it at home.

Method Three: Out-annoy them. The idea is to escalate every annoying thing they say. For example, if they say "I'm a Republican and I believe we should have guns!" You respond with "Damn right we should have guns! How else are we going to launch the revolution? In fact, we're having a meeting tomorrow night; and you're just the kind of person we're looking for! By the way, what's your blood type?"

Costumes work, too.

The Art of Experimentation

If you do a quick search on the Interwebz, you'll find a tremendous number of ultramarathon training tips and advice. You'll find dozens of training plans, philosophies, techniques, and research. You'll also find a ton of information refuting each and every one of those training plans, philosophies, techniques, and research.

What does this mean?

There is no one right answer.

You can follow a lot of different plans and still get to the finish line. You can even make up your own plan out of thin air. It does help to have some guidance though, so how do you choose? I gave some common options earlier. Many are tempted to just do what their favorite elite runner does. This will probably work, but that elite, like every other runner, is a different individual. Their plan probably isn't the best fit for you.

I'll discuss a large number of ideas to consider, from training plans to the tiny details of ultrarunning. I would highly recommend developing your own process of experimentation to decide how to deal with each issue. Test out a wide variety of ideas. Keep those that work. Get rid of those that do not. By using this process, you will continually improve using the methods that work best for you.

In essence, think of your ultramarathon training as one huge experiment, and you're the subject.

Here's the method:

Step One: Choose the new thing to test. It may be a food, piece of gear, exercise, what lube prevents your junk from chafing... whatever. Only change one variable at a time.

Step Two: Test the new variable. In many cases, this will involve going for a run. Pay close attention to the effects of the variable. If it is a food, how did it make you feel? Was it easy to eat? Is it something that can be carried with you?

Step Three: Decide if the variable helped, hurt, or further experimentation is needed. If it seemed to help, adopt it as part of the training. If it hurt, abandon it. If further testing is needed, try it again.

This simple process can be used to tailor a training plan to your needs and abilities.

Speedwork

There are a few types of runs that make up most training plans. The first I'll discuss is speedwork. As the name implies, speedwork involves running really fast. Different people have different ideas of what exactly constitutes speedwork. I'm going with a simple definition:

Any run where talking is extremely difficult.

Speedwork helps make you faster. There aren't too many times you'll need speed in ultras, especially your first. I recommend speedwork to prevent you from getting slower over time. Long-term ultrarunners that only run long, slow distances usually experience a degree of muscle atrophy and loss of speed. Occasionally running fast helps prevent that.

Speedwork can take several forms. Some people like running repeats, or laps around a track. Others like to do tempo runs, which are shorter, faster runs. I prefer running short races, like 5ks or add a sprinting component to my crosstraining. I'm not a huge fan of fast running, so I've used some various "motivational" methods over the years.

My favorite method involved sprinting down sand hills. It was easy, fun, and made me feel *really* fast.

The worst method involved an evil workout called a Tabata. It involved sprinting for 30 seconds, walking for 20, then repeating that cycle eight times. I'd rest for a few seconds, then do it again. I repeated the eight cycles six times. I threw up twice. It wouldn't have been so bad if it weren't for the Taco Bell spicy burrito I ate a few hours before.

Fartleks

A Fartlek run is a run where your speed is going to vary for random distances. Sometimes you run fast, sometimes you run slow. The distance is usually relatively short, maybe a few miles.

You should do Fartlek runs for no other reason than the name. It's fun to say "I'm going out to do a Fartlek!"

If you need more justification, you should do them because they train your body to make the adjustment from running fast to running slow to walking and back. In an ultra, you'll probably make this transition several (if not many) times. This training run will help.

You also get some of the benefits of speedwork without as much "vomit" danger. When you begin to reach that threshold, you just slow down.

Hill Repeats

Hill repeats involve running up and down hills, usually at a high intensity. I love hill repeats. In my experience, it's the single most effective type of ultramarathon training. You develop strength from running up hill and speed from running down hill.

When we lived in Michigan, our hill-repeat workouts were done on an old garbage pile-turned ski hill. It was like visiting Disney World with Mickey handing out free bacon. Since we didn't have too many large hills, we would do multiple repeats for each workout. Sand dunes along the pristine shore of Lake Michigan also made for a good hill-repeat workout.

Since we've been traveling around, we've had the opportunity to run up and down a lot of mountain trails. This usually results in a single run up and down without multiple repeats. Either method works.

If you live in an area that has no hills, you could get some of the same effect by running up and down the stairs of skyscrapers. Or you could run up and down parking garages. If you have a treadmill, you can set the incline to simulate uphill running. If the treadmill has a foldable deck, you can prop up the back to simulate downhill running. Just don't fall.

Tip- if you are running a race that features hills, do hill repeats! My first trail marathon was run on a hilly course. I didn't do any hill repeats. By mile 18, I couldn't walk up the hills forward. I had to do a sort of side-stepping shuffle. It sucked. Worse, I was passed by a lady in her late sixties doing her first-ever race.

The Long Run

Be honest. You probably thought I skimped on the last few explanations of the other training runs. It's because most ultrarunners don't do them. They spend most of their time and energy focusing on the centerpiece of every training plan- the long run.

Well, except for CFE. If that was your training run selection, go ahead and skip this part. CFE frowns on the logic behind the long, slow run so you never have the opportunity to learn the subtle nuances of covering long distances. Just don't bitch to me after your 50 miler when your ass crack gets severely chafed, then the cheeks fuse together as they heal. It really happens. Google it.

Okay, where was I? Oh yeah, the long run. The long run serves two purposes:

First, trains your body to deal with the rigors of running long distances. You accomplish this by increasing your long run distance gradually over time. It strengthens your muscles, tendons, ligaments, bones, endocrine system, and any other bodily system that's stressed over long distances.

Second, it allows you to experiment in conditions that are at least somewhat similar to race conditions. How is that water bottle going to feel after 24 miles? Will those packets of spaghetti-flavored Gu still taste good after eight hours of running? Can you bend over to tie your shoes after 32 miles? How about needing to squat to drop a deuce? You can't test these variables without the long run.

Long runs can take on a few different flavors. You could do one single long, continuous run. You could do two shorter runs over two days. You could do five or six shorter runs over the course of one day. Different plans will use one of the different flavors. Personally I like to do all three, though I use the first more than the last two.

When I design my own plans, I like to schedule a run that is long enough for me to develop an "ultra hurt." I want to experience the point where the pain starts getting annoying; the point where I have to start actively dealing with it. This usually comes at about the 25-30 mile distance.

The longest training run I've ever done is the infamous Kal-Haven double crossing in SW Michigan. Jesse Scott, Mark Robillard, and I set out on a 68 mile out-and-back on a 34 mile rails-to-trails path. It sucked. We had a friend, Tony Schaub, riding a bike to carry some of our gear, but it did little to dampen the extreme beating our bodies took. It definitely crossed the "this run is too long to produce a positive training effect, and will likely just hurt us" threshold. I ran a 100 miler three weeks later and definitely suffered more than I should have. It set me up for a serious case of overtraining that shelved me for months.

The lesson- long training runs are important learning tools. *REALLY* long training runs are stupid.

Crosstraining

We're preparing to run a race. As such, we should run. Right?

Not always. Many new ultrarunners make the mistake of focusing entirely on running and ignoring any other form of exercise.

The problem?

If you do nothing but run, you'll likely develop muscle imbalances, which may lead to injury. It can also increase flexibility, muscle endurance, and recovery. It will also prepare your body for some of the unexpected elements of ultras. For example, the weight training I do

105

helps me carry my water bottle for the duration of races. That 20 ounce bottle of water gets quite heavy after 100 miles.

So what are the options?

Pretty much any non-running exercise will be effective crosstraining. Here are some ideas:

- Mountain biking
- Yoga
- Kickboxing
- Unicycling (thanks Rob Youngren)
- Weight training
- Competing in the Lumberjack Games
- Testing the entire Kama Sutra
- Swimming
- MMA training

If you want one specific recommendation, I suggest functional fitness-high intensity interval training. What the Hell is that? It combines exercises that utilize a wide variety of muscle groups with workout formats that make you sweat. A lot.

Crossfit is usually viewed as a form of functional fitness. P90X is another popular program. If I were to give a specific recommendation, I'd suggest Pete Kemme's workouts that can be found at http://kemmefitness.com. His workouts range from mild to extreme, so they appeal to beginners, experts, and everyone in between. One of his more famous workouts involved doing a burpee then leaping forward... for a mile. He's also fond of using homemade gym equipment like slosh tubes, doing weird "animal walks" up and down stairs, and creating 1,000 ways to do a pushup. Pete's crazy workouts helped me finish all of my 100 milers.

I would recommend doing a crosstraining activity at least twice per week. Don't be afraid to mix it up. Any physical activity other than running will help train you for ultras.

Course Specificity Training

If you have the opportunity to practice on the ultra course, take it!
Being familiar with the course is a huge advantage. Not only do you
learn the useful information like aid station locations and potential
trouble spots, but you will be developing the running skills needed to
tackle that specific race. You'll learn to run through the specific rocks,
roots, mud holes, and hills that litter the course.

In the event you cannot run the same course, try to find a place to train
that is as similar to the course as possible. Match up things like altitude,
elevation change, surface (hard packed dirt, gravel, sand, rock, etc.)

Early in my ultra career, I rarely had the opportunity to train on the
course I was planning on running. I did go to great lengths to find
comparable trails, though. This usually involved scouring YouTube and
Google Images for any visuals I could find. It also involved reading as
many race reports as I could find.

Some variables are nearly impossible to experience, like altitude. When
I trained for Western States (with a maximum altitude of 11,000 feet), I
needed at way to simulate the lack of oxygen I'd experience. I lived in
Michigan, which has an altitude of about 500 ft above sea level. The
solution- I did several runs while breathing through a drinking straw

from McDonald's. While I doubt it did anything physiologically, it did teach me a valuable lesson: There was a definite connection between available oxygen and pace. I quickly learned to be especially conservative and take frequent walk breaks. I also learned our local police department is suspicious of dudes running barefoot at night while breathing through a straw. What's weird about that?

Periodization

Periodization is a process of preparing for ultras by building specific skills at specific times. It usually begins with an endurance base-building phase, followed by a hill climbing and descending phase (or strength training), and followed by a speed-building phase.

The idea works fairly well. By introducing each concept separately, you can develop each skill faster than if you were to do all three simultaneously. You begin with the most general skills (running long distances). As your goal race nears, you hone the specific skills needed for the ultra.

I used a system of periodization for my first ultra. I spent 12 weeks building my endurance base, 6 weeks working on speed, and 6 weeks working on specific trails. Note I didn't do any hill training. It was a huge mistake. The hills on the course absolutely killed me. Live and learn.

Losing Weight for Race Day

Should you try to lose weight prior to race day? It depends. Generally-speaking, the less you weigh, the more efficient you become. If you're at a healthy body weight, I would not recommend losing more. If you are overweight, trying to drop a few pounds might help you get to the finish line.

Due to my love of food and beer, I regularly pack on anywhere from 15 to 25 extra pounds between races. As my goal races approach, I usually try to cut that down a bit. I've found my ideal race weight to be around 175-180 pounds (I'm six feet tall).

I find the natural process of training usually takes care of the added weight. As my weekly running and crosstraining increases, my caloric expenditure surpasses my caloric intake.

If that doesn't work, I fall back on the greatest weight loss secret in the world: I deliberately eat less and move more. But I don't give up candy. Or beer.

Should you lose weight? I'd recommend a few simple tests:

For the guys: Strip down naked. Reach your arms above your head. Look down. Can you see your penis? Don't cheat- erections don't count. If you can, you're good. If you can't, you might consider losing a few pounds prior to the race.

For the ladies [from Shelly]: Designate a pair of your "A" pants. You know, the pants that you know make your ass look great. If they fit, you're right where you want to be. If they're tight, lose a few pounds.

Race Etiquette

There are a few unwritten rules of racing. Most runners learn these lessons by experience... mostly by inadvertently breaking the rules. This becomes a little more complicated because road races and trail races have slightly different etiquette. Here are the major trail race "rules":

Start in a Position Relative to Your Pace

Trails are often congested at the beginning of trail races due to a large number of people funneling down relatively narrow trails. Start in a position relative to your ability. If you're fast, start near the front. If you're slow, start near the back. If you plan on walking at the start (not uncommon for 100 milers), start at the very back.

Passing

Passing rules are based on the commonly-held trail traffic guidelines (tips from Mark Norfleet and Jacobus Degroot).

- **Passing a slower runner:** Since trail races are commonly held on single track trails, passing etiquette is important. As a general rule, always pass on the left. Announce you're about to pass by saying "passing on the left." Thank the person you pass. Build good karma by wishing them luck.
- **Getting passed by a faster runner:** Always yield to someone faster. If someone approaches from behind and asks to pass, either step off to the right side of the trail or move as far right as possible. Again, wish them good luck.
- **On hills:** The person going uphill always has the right of way, so the person going down should yield and allow them to pass. However, I make an exception if the downhill runner is a faster runner. On an out-and-back course, it's common for a mid-pack runner like me to meet the leaders as they're coming back from the turn-around point. If I'm going up and they're coming down, I'll yield to them.
- **Non-racers:** If you encounter non-racers, the same trail rules apply. Always yield to vehicles, mounted animals, and pack animals. Mountain bikers are supposed to yield to runners, but be careful. In my experience, only about half of all mountain bikers actually follow that rule.

Littering

Littering is not acceptable under any circumstance. In road races, it's common for runners to toss their cups, empty gel packets, or other crap on the ground after an aid station or along the course under the assumption that the race volunteers will clean up their mess. In trail races, this behavior is strictly forbidden. In fact, some race directors are beginning to automatically disqualify those that litter. I applaud their efforts. Keep nature beautiful and don't expect volunteers to clean up after your sloppy ass.

Treat Volunteers with the Respect They Deserve

Volunteers are donating their time for YOU. Don't yell at them, berate them, or insult them. Not all volunteers will be experienced ultrarunners, so don't get upset if they make a mistake or can't fulfill your every request. When leaving an aid station, thank the volunteers for donating their time.

Don't Complain

This is a tough thing for some chronic complainers, but the rest of us would appreciate it. Don't complain about trivial matters like aid station food selection, volunteers, the race director, the difficulty of the course, weather, etc. Trail racing is supposed to be a challenge. If you're not up for the challenge and unpredictability of a trail race, stay at home.

Pooping

If you have to drop a deuce during the race, move off the trail. The terrain usually determines the distance, but 20 feet should be considered a minimum. Also, try to get behind some sort of visual barrier. It's never cool to round a corner and catch a glimpse of someone pinching a loaf trailside.

On a semi-related note- don't grab aid station food with the same hand used to wipe. (tip from Jason Griffith)

Music

Many runners prefer to listen to music while running. If you choose to listen to music, please have the decency to use headphones. I don't want to listen to Taylor Swift rant about the angst caused by a breakup she initiated at mile 60 of an ultra. If you are using headphones, keep the volume low so you can hear other runners trying to pass (tip from Kelsey Gray, Jocelyn Anderson, and Caleb Wilson). Alternatively, you can leave one ear bud out (tip from Vanessa Rodriguez.)

Spitting and Snot Rockets

If you have to spit or blow a snot rocket, make sure nobody is in the line of fire. Be sure you take the wind into account (tip from Louie Auslander).

Obstacles

If you have to move a branch out of the way, don't let it snap back on the person immediately behind you (tip from Krista Cavendar). Also, warn people behind you of any major obstacle on the trail like deep holes, huge rocks, rattlesnakes, ill-placed dookie, etc. (tip from Caleb Wilson). Use your discretion, though. There's no need to blurt out every single irregularity.

Trail Markings

Trail markings are the objects used to mark a course. Since trail races are usually run in areas with multiple intersecting trails, the trail markings are necessary to keep runners on the right track. The most common materials used are ribbons, glow sticks (at night), signs, and ground markings. Different races use different markings depending on terrain, environment, and availability of volunteers to mark the course. It's important to attend pre-race meetings and read course descriptions to determine how the course will be marked and what materials will be used.

In some cases, trail markings may be removed intentionally or unintentionally by other trail users. It's also possible for animals to eat the markings. At the Bighorn 100 miler, it's not uncommon for elk to eat the ribbons used for marking.

When running any race, pay attention to markings instead of blindly following other runners. Race directors will usually give an approximate distance between markers. If you cover significantly more than that distance and don't see a marker, there's a good chance you went off course. Backtrack until you find the last marker, and then continue on from there.

Runner Personalities

As runners, most of us fit in one of two categories:

#1: We strive to improve our abilities, or
#2: We accept our abilities and focus on the enjoyment of running.

The vast majority of runners will be some combination of these two extremes, but will be a little closer to one side or the other.

Both approaches have distinct advantages and disadvantages. If you strive to improve your abilities, you'll actually improve your running skills. You'll be able to run longer, faster, or both. You'll likely identify weaknesses in your running abilities and take steps to improve. There are downsides, too. You may never feel quite satisfied. You could have always run a little faster or longer, or there will always be someone that does a little better. If you're not chasing authentic goals (goals YOU set as opposed to goals that are set for us by others), you may end up with a hollow sense of accomplishment. Lastly, you may look down on other runners that don't share the desire to constantly improve.

The "running for enjoyment" personality has advantages, too. You're likely going to play to your strengths. If you're a road runner, you'll stick to roads. You're also more likely to be happy with your current situation. You don't need to accomplish anything to feel good about yourself. Lastly, you'll be more likely to accept others for the runners they are without judging their abilities or performances. There are downsides to this mindset, too. You may feel like you're not really accomplishing anything. You may feel your approach is just an excuse to be a lazy ass. You may shun others because they try to be competitive or improve regularly. Finally you may not be good advocates for the sport.

As you can probably guess, extremes of either are not good. Striking a happy balance somewhere in between would probably be the ideal.

Race Strategy

How do you plan for a race measured in hours? I will sometimes overhear runners discussing 5K strategy. It usually involves running at a specified intensity for various intervals with the goal of finishing as quickly as possible. Personally, I've always used a "run as fast as you can" strategy... which may explain why I suck at 5Ks. Anyway, I digress.

Needless to say, ultramarathons require a different strategy than the faster, shorter races. Even a typical marathon strategy won't necessarily be effective. Important note- I'm assuming you are not planning on winning the ultra; your goal is to finish. Lazy runners don't plan to win.

Before we delve into detail, there are a few universal differences between ultras and sub-ultras. The longer the ultra, the greater this difference.

1   Walking is acceptable. Only the elites will run the entire time.

2   Eating *during* the run is more or less required.

3   Ultras are about surviving... you always have to assess the cumulative effects of your decisions. A bad decision early in a race will haunt you throughout.

Okay, now we tackle strategy.

The first thing to consider: The distance. Generally speaking, longer races require more walking. In a 50 mile race, you may walk a total of 10 miles. In a 100 mile race, you may walk 40-50 miles.

The second consideration: Cutoff times. Most races will set an absolute time before everyone packs up and goes home. Most races will require you to meet certain time checkpoints. If you fall behind these checkpoints, you will be removed from the race.

The third consideration: Terrain. A flat course will require a much different strategy than a mountainous course. When assessing terrain, it is also useful to note the different obstacles you will encounter. Will the course consist of asphalt? Dirt trails? Sand? Lots of rocks and/or roots (technical trail?) Stairs? Steep hills? It is easier to run faster on certain surfaces; this will play a role in planning.

The fourth consideration: Fitness. The greater your fitness level, the faster and longer you will be able to run. Personally, I usually overestimate my fitness level. I am slowly learning how my body will react to long distances, which results in a better plan.

The fifth consideration: Aid stations. The time does not stop while you're gorging yourself on M&Ms and salted potatoes. The time spent in aid stations will affect your overall finish time. As such, it is necessary to factor this into planning. I like to plan on a five minute stop at each aid station. I tell my crew to keep the stops under one minute. Depending on how much primping I need, my time usually falls between those two times.

The sixth consideration: Slowing as the race progresses. Remember, you're a lazy runner. You won't be running negative splits in an ultra. Assume your second half pace will be significantly slower than the first half pace.

The seventh consideration: Weather. Some conditions, such as heavy rain (and subsequent mud), snow, high heat, oppressive humidity, or strong winds can slow you down. It is important to estimate the climate and local weather before developing a race strategy.

The last consideration: Strategy. Now that you have done the requisite research, you will be prepared to map out a strategy. How exactly you devise that plan will depend on your organizational habits. I like to estimate a variety of finish times with the elapsed time I would expect to reach each aid station. Once the calculations are made, I print a chart. If weather is expected to be wet, I laminate it. It takes some work, but it gives me an easy-to-follow spreadsheet that I can use during the race to determine if I am going too slow or too fast.

Warning: *Make sure your crew understands your chart.* Luckily, my first 100 mile finish was helped significantly by Michael Helton's ability to interpret my laminated poster board filled with mileage numbers and times. Michael deciphered this between rushing from one aid station to the next. It would have been wise to explain my system *before* the race started.

I find it is easier if I don't plan walk breaks. In my first 100 mile attempt, I had planned every single walk break throughout the race. Not only was it incredibly time-consuming, it was impossible to follow once the race started. It served as a major distraction. Some runners will use a specific time ratio to determine walking breaks. I have experimented with this idea extensively and was never able to find a good solution that worked well. Now I use more of a Zen-like approach and walk when I feel like it.

The race strategy you map out will go a long way towards preventing the unexpected. Still, the more potential problems you can anticipate, the greater the likelihood of finishing.

Overplanning can be dangerous, too. You cannot predict every single issue that may arise. Some problems require you to fix them as they arise. Experience will improve those problem-solving abilities, as will long training runs.

Run/Walk Strategy

Walking during races? By now, you probably understand the necessity of walking. For ultrarunners, it's often a requirement to finish. For new runners, it's the preferred method to build endurance. For serious road runners, it's considered a mortal sin. But it's rarely something we practice.

Jeff Galloway has made a living coaching runners to use a run-walk strategy when racing... and it really works! The idea is simple- by interspersing walking breaks with periods of running, you can run faster and cut time off your finishes. Galloway has published a ton of books to help guide runners to the finish line using the run-walk-run method.

You don't necessarily need a book, though. I prefer to use the run-walk-run method based on feel. I run until I need a break, then walk until I feel recovered enough to run again. Then repeat.

I don't do this in training too often, but I DO like to work on fast walking skills. Since we see the walk break as a rest period, we tend to stroll along at a leisurely pace. Unfortunately, this wastes a lot of time. If we can cut our walking pace from 20:00 minute miles down to around 10-12 minute miles, we'll dramatically improve our finish times while still benefiting from the recovery periods afforded by the walk breaks.

Much like speed training for running, speed training for walking will make your "cruising speed" more comfortable.

So How Do You Get Faster?

Luckily, becoming a faster walker is much easier than becoming a fast runner. It's more about learning technique than actually improving aerobic or anaerobic conditioning.

I recommend two different workouts, each done once per week.

Workout one: Walk as fast as you can for two or three miles. This is a sustained effort. Try to maintain as fast of a pace as possible without breaking into a running gait.

Workout two: Alternate between walking fast and running. Again, I recommend a two to three mile route. Start by walking a quarter mile, then run at a slow pace for a quarter mile. Repeat for the entire distance.

Since neither of these workouts are high-impact, they can be added to whatever routine you're currently doing. If needed, adjust the distance. Personally I haven't found much benefit to walking more than 2-3 miles in one session, so it's not a workout that will grow longer with experience.

Walking Technique?

Many people, especially barefoot and minimalist shoe runners, ask about walking technique. Do you land heel-toe or toe-heel?

I alter my technique based on terrain. On flat, smooth terrain, I use the heel-toe technique with slightly longer steps. On rough terrain, I shortened my stride and use a toe-heel technique (much like I do when running).

Since walking produces only a fraction of the ground reaction force of running, use whatever technique feels most comfortable.

Speeding Up Strategy

The following section was a blog post I wrote about my initial experimentation with speeding up when tired. I had been doing mostly slow trail running, but was worried about a timed race on asphalt in the near future. Since this first experiment, I've successfully used the strategy in every ultra I've run.

This post was inspired by a 34 mile training run with Jesse Scott. We're training for the Mind the Ducks 12 Hour ultra in Rochester, NY. To help prepare us trail runners prepare for half a day on asphalt, we decided to run on a paved bike path.

At about mile 20, Jesse decided to mix things up a bit by adding the occasional "speed up." At a specific landmark, we'd essentially start sprinting until we reached another landmark. The distances varied from about 50 meters to 100 meters or so. Our pace throughout the run was in the ballpark of 9-9:45 minute miles; the sprint pace was probably about 5:15 for Jesse and 6:40 for me. It was a good method to add interest to an otherwise tortuous run.

I noticed something else, too. Even though it was tough to initiate the sprint, the sprint itself felt shockingly *good*. After we slowed down, my muscles felt loose and free. I was able to cruise at a faster pace. My mood improved. I was shocked that I felt great, even after 20+ miles on roads. We ended up doing seven or eight of these "speed ups" in fairly rapids succession.

Between speed ups, we talked about the typical walking strategy used in ultras. Many runners will begin walking at a very early pace to conserve energy to perform better later in the race. I tried this strategy in my early ultra days but found it didn't work for me. I slowed my overall pace to the point where cut-offs became an issue. It also didn't seem to delay the point of extreme fatigue.

I found a more effective strategy was to run as long as I could, then add walk breaks when necessary. Note- I walk uphills the entire course for anything over a 50k. This resulted in a pretty good improvement in finish times.

I still had a problem, though. Once I started walking, the transition from running to walking and back would be painful. I didn't get much relief from walking, and it killed my pace once I started running again. In essence, walking made me feel *worse*.

After this last experiment with speed ups, I think I may try implementing this in my races. **Instead of walking, I will try speeding up instead of taking walk breaks.** I have to find the ideal ratio of speed ups. Jesse and I did one about every half mile, which was far too often. I may start at every 2-3 miles and observe the results. It defies conventional wisdom, but I've had a great deal of success doing the opposite of everybody else.

Logic seems to predict this idea will be an abysmal failure. It would seem as though the strategy would be excessively taxing on your body. Or would it? From a physiological standpoint, I can't hypothesize what effects this has. Would the net effects be better or worse?

My optimism toward this strategy stems from seeing it in action. The strategy has worked very well for Jesse. During the_Woodstock 50 miler, he dramatically sped up whenever he hit gravel roads. He won the race by about an hour. I also cannot deny the effect it had on our run. I felt MUCH better after our speedup than after stopping to eat.

Tapering

Tapering is the process of resting prior to running a race. The idea is to train hard for a period of time, then give your body a chance to fully heal before you hit the start line. There are several schools of thought regarding tapering.

Some advocate a long, drawn-out taper where you slowly ramp down mileage and intensity. A common strategy is to begin the taper about a month before the race by reducing your training volume by about fifty percent each week, then eliminating running completely in the week immediately before the race. I used this strategy for my first three years of ultrarunning. Since my body wasn't quite adapted to the rigors of ultrarunning, it worked fairly well. I was healthy, but felt a little rusty for the first half of the race.

Eventually I moved toward the second school of thought- utilizing a very limited taper. I would maintain a normal training routine until about three days before a race, then do short "shake-out" runs each day. This strategy worked well because I didn't feel rusty the morning of the race.

Most beginners could probably utilize a middle ground strategy. Unless you're injured, there's not much of a need to taper for four weeks. Two weeks should be adequate for almost everyone. As you gain more experience, you can shorten the length of the taper.

Fasting while Training

Many of my ultra friends have started experimenting with low heart rate training. The technique is based on the idea that we can train our body to run faster while remaining in an aerobic zone (burning fat versus carbs as a primary fuel). Many people have had success with the method. I've played around with the idea, but found the long, slow running to be too boring. *It took the fun out of running.*

For years, I've used a *different* technique that accomplishes a similar task. I purposely fast about 12 to 24 hours before some of my long runs, then do not eat during the run. This forces glycogen depletion very early in the run. As a result, my body burns its available stockpile of carbs. At first, the crash is severe. It's what marathoners like to call "the wall." My average pace decreases dramatically and I feel terrible. After a few such runs, the crash becomes a lot less severe and I'm able to maintain a much faster post-crash pace. Furthermore, the subjective feeling evolves from "horrible" to "eh, this isn't too bad." In essence, I'm training my body to deal with glycogen depletion and utilize fat as a primary fuel source.

With low heart rate training, the goal is to increase your aerobic pace to decrease finish times. This works well if you remain under that aerobic threshold, or the point where your body is using mostly fat as fuel, for the entire race. Personally I don't like to have that limitation. I like the freedom of adjusting my pace based on how I feel, the terrain, available food, competition… whatever.

Low heart rate training teaches your body to utilize fat as a fuel, which allows you to run faster while using more fat and less glycogen. Regularly training on an empty stomach does something similar. Check out these articles:

Piece of evidence #1:
http://www.marathonguide.com/training/articles/MandBFuelOnFat.cfm

Piece of evidence #2: http://www.ncbi.nlm.nih.gov/pubmed/20452283

The Elite Question

People sometimes ask how elite ultrarunners race while consuming very little food. Here's an example. At the Bighorn Ultra in 2012, Damian Stoy, the 50 mile overall winner, ran the race on *three* gels. That's roughly 300 calories. He would have burned between 5,000-6,000 calories for the entire race. Assuming he started with about 2,000 calories worth of glycogen (stored in muscles and the liver), he would have had at least a 2,700 calorie deficit over the course of the race. Most of those 2,700 calories had to come from fat.

How is it he could have maintained a winning pace (9:22) over rugged terrain with lots of climbing while fighting a glycogen deficit? He had to rely on fat as fuel. But he clearly wasn't running below his aerobic threshold (he was breathing hard when he passed me).

I would hypothesize that he does what most fast runners tend to do- *eat very little before and during training runs.*

Sidebar- Damian is an accomplished ChiRunning coach. If you are in need of running form coaching, look him up. Dude knows his shit.

What Would I Recommend?

Low heart rate training is an invaluable tool... for building a good endurance base. The low intensity dramatically decreases recovery time and limits the occurrence of injuries. I highly recommend new runners use this method to build an endurance base regardless of your goal distances.

Once you build that base, however, low heart rate training is of little value. The slow pace will limit your speed. Doing speedwork like fartlek runs, tempo runs, and interval training will help make you faster. If you're planning to run anything over a half marathon, adding foodless training will continue to develop your ability to use fat as fuel.

121

This will limit the negative effects of the "wall" that cripples so many runners.

Let's look at a typical marathoner. Most marathon training plans top out at around 20-22 mile long runs. If a marathoner eats before a long run of that distance, it's unlikely they will experience glycogen depletion during training. When running the actual race, they cross that line of glycogen depletion during those last few miles. Since it's something their body rarely if ever experiences, it hits hard. Really, really hard.

You can eliminate this problem using a few methods:

1. Run the entire race below your aerobic threshold so you burn mostly fat. This would be the strategy recommended by the low heart rate crowd. The problem- you're forced to stay below that threshold or you'll hit 'the wall."
2. Eat enough to cover the deficit. In the case of a marathon, consuming 300 to 800 calories before or during the race will be enough to supply enough calories to cover that deficit. Personally I like this strategy, but it will fail if you can't eat enough to cover the distance.
3. Train to run despite the wall. By training regularly on an empty stomach and purposely hitting the wall, you'll limit the negative effects of glycogen depletion.

The best-case scenario would be to utilize all three. Build an endurance base using low heart rate training. During the race, eat if you can. If you can't, your foodless training will guarantee performance won't be impeded by a glycogen crash.

The Actual Training

I try to use this method at least twice per week. It's pretty easy- just run long enough to deplete your glycogen stores. The longer you fast before your run, the earlier you'll crash. If I eat immediately before a run, I'll usually hit the wall around mile 18-20. If I fast for 12 hours, it usually hits around 13-15. If I fast for 24 hours, I may hit the wall within the first 5-8 miles. Your results will vary. Once you hit the crash, continue running for a few miles without eating. I aim for about four to five miles.

The first few times are going to be awful. Your pace will decrease dramatically. You'll feel drained. Stuff will hurt. You'll probably feel depressed. Don't worry- all of these symptoms will ease after a few training sessions. Eventually the "crash" barely registers. Furthermore, each subsequent crash experienced in the same run is lessened. In an ultra, this is important because most people decide to drop from races while in the middle of an especially bad low point. Make the low points more tolerable and your finish rate increases.

This method also teaches you to predict when glycogen depletion is about to occur. You'll learn the subtle, often-missed early signs mentioned in the previous paragraph. In a race, these signs can be used as a cue to eat something, thus preventing the crash before it becomes worse.

I like to do these training sessions a few months before my goal race. Four or five sessions seems to produce good results. Eight to ten sessions seems to maximize the effect.

Conclusion

Training on an empty stomach can be an invaluable tool to your training if you plan to run longer races. It's not difficult (though mildly unpleasant in the beginning). The potential benefits can be huge as it frees you from the shackles of maintaining an aerobic-zone pace and regular food consumption. Personally this method has been instrumental in my own training for 100 mile races.

Gluttony Training

Before I get to the details, I should note this training really only applies to ultrarunners. Most people should be able to run anything up to about 18-20 miles without any food. Even a marathon would require very little food, if any at all. Once you pass that marathon threshold, food becomes increasingly important as distance increases.

Many runners hit a point during a race where they simply cannot stomach any food. Either they don't have an appetite or the taste/smell of food makes them nauseous. As a result, they stop eating. This leads to a glycogen/depletion crash. That often leads to a DNF.

The solution is simple- *train to eat.*

This is what I do. Approximately once every two or three weeks, I'll eat a fairly large meal about 30 minutes before a long run. My preferred meal is a Quarter-Pounder extra value meal. If you're fast food-averse, any food will work... just make sure it's voluminous. On the same run, eat something about every 30 minutes. I'd shoot for 100 calories in the beginning, and slowly work up to 200-300 on subsequent runs. I like to experiment with the actual food to help figure out what foods I can tolerate. As the distance increases, your tastes will likely change.

This is invaluable information as it will help you pack drop bags for future ultras. Eventually you'll probably find a few foods that work in all situations. I always like to have these foods on-hand in races. My all-purpose foods are:

- Chia seeds
- Slim-Fast
- Turkey and cheese sandwiches
- Mashed potatoes

I can eat all four in any condition (i.e. they never make me nauseous). The key to this training is to go slow. If you feel like vomiting (which is normal in the beginning), slow down to a walk. Speed up when you feel better.

So what exactly are the benefits of this training?

- Appears to help teach your body to digest food better while running, which allows you to consume more calories per hour if and when it's needed
- Teaches you which foods you can tolerate while running
- Teaches you the skill of physically putting food in your mouth while moving
- Allows you to occasionally indulge in foods with little guilt (important for my foodie friends)
- Helps you develop a feel for how much you can eat and still perform well (too little = crash, too much = nausea)

I'd put this specific training method in the category of "unorthodox." However, it is effective. When I started running, I couldn't even eat a gel. Now I could consume a Thanksgiving dinner. This specific skill is easy to develop and has become a relative strength in races. I find it's usually better to eat too little instead of too much, but I know I can quickly and easily recover from a caloric-deficit if needed. It's a handy tool to have in the toolbox.

Thermoregulation

Early in 2012 I wrote a post about some difficulties I had in hot, dry weather., I theorized about the role a moisture-wicking shirt played in three crappy runs over a period of several months. After reading the comments from my audience and doing a little research, I came to an obvious conclusion:

Moisture-wicking clothing does more harm than good for runners in hot, dry weather.

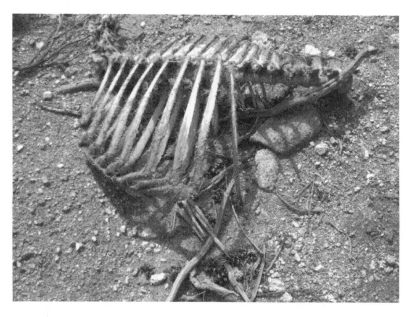

The reasoning is simple- the mechanism of drawing moisture away from the skin thwarts the process of evaporative cooling of sweat. In other words, the wicking of the moisture means the sweat evaporates on the surface of the shirt, not your skin, so we're robbing our body of one of the primary cooling mechanisms used to reduce our core body temperature.

The marketing material from several moisture wicking companies confirms this. They are very guarded about saying the fabric cools you down in heat. Instead, they tend to use statements like "the fabric makes you feel more comfortable." Indeed, moisture wicking fabrics are great... when you're not generating a ton of heat via exercise.

My rule of thumb- I'm only using moisture-wicking fabric in cold weather or in warmer weather when my activity level is low enough where body temps can be maintained without the sweating mechanism. If I am running in hot weather, I'm going with loose-fitting white cotton or no shirt at all.

Sidebar- the shirtless option may also have another benefit- *prevention of internal cancers*. Check out this article:

http://www.innerself.com/Health/cancer_sun.htm

Note the citation from Dr. Gordy Ainsleigh. We did a run with Gordy during the summer of 2012 and he was, of course, shirtless.

Thermoregulation: My Missing Link

I did a lot of experimenting with perceived body temperature and how it makes me feel. I believe my problems at Bighorn in 2012, a disastrous Boulder to Nederland, Colorado run in 2012, and the 2011-2012 Across the Years race were all caused by overheating.

During each of those events, I knew heat was the problem... indirectly. I assumed I wasn't drinking enough (dehydration) or I wasn't taking enough electrolyte supplementation (hyponatremia.) These are the two often-quoted causes of the symptoms I was experiencing. In fact, most runners recommended either drinking more or taking more electrolytes.

The feelings I was having weren't quite right, though. In training, I have purposely run to a point of dehydration. Early in my running "career", I also experienced the early signs of hyponatremia. Neither of these feelings were quite the same. There was some other variable I was missing.

That variable was a rising core body temperature.

Generally I'm a pretty good hot weather runner. I can tolerate heat far better than cold. In the humid Midwest, I used to run on the hottest of days with no issues at all. I didn't experience this problem until I started running in hot, *dry* weather... and then only when wearing moisture-wicking shirts.

As I explained previously, the moisture wicking material apparently caused my core temperature to rise faster than my sweating mechanism (and passive heat-dissipation methods) could get rid of the excess. The result was extreme fatigue, dizziness, and severe cramping, all of which can be explained with Noakes' "central governor" theory- my body was fighting me to stop moving to prevent, well, death.

In all three cases, I didn't have signs of dehydration or hyponatremia. As such, drinking more or consuming electrolytes had no effect. What *did* help, however, was getting out of the sun and stopping activity. THAT allowed my core temperature to cool.

Some basic experiments seem to support this theory. I did two runs up a mountain. The mountain had several "micro-climates" of various combinations of sun exposure and wind. The goal was to try to replicate the feelings of fatigue, dizziness, and cramping without having to run a crazy long distance. I accomplished this by running at a strenuous pace up the mountain. I made sure I was adequately hydrated and electrolytes were supplemented before the run to help rule those out as confounding variables. I carried one water bottle and drank to thirst throughout the run, which equaled about 12 ounces per hour.

The Results

I was able to mimic the exact same feelings I had in the three disastrous runs, though to a lesser degree. The symptoms were worse in sun-exposed areas with no wind, improved in the sun-exposed areas with wind and shaded areas with no wind, and completely disappeared in shaded areas with wind.

I was shocked the results were so clear. Previously, I was at a complete loss as to the cause of the symptoms because I didn't consider body temperature to be a variable. It was never an issue in years of prior running, even when air temps were very high.

As soon as I recognized body temperature as a variable, the correlations became obvious. If sweat isn't cooling me down, performance suffers. A lot.

The Solution

The solutions are obvious. I have to work on methods to stay cool. Here are the steps I will take:

- **Train in heat more often.** Theoretically, this will help make the body's thermoregulation system more efficient. At the very least, it will help train me to recognize the early signs of overheating.
- **In hot, dry weather, go shirtless.** This will maximize evaporative cooling.
- **If there's a lot of sun exposure, wear white cotton shirts.** The white cotton will absorb less heat than skin. The cotton, when saturated with sweat, will allow evaporative cooling via conduction. I don't think it is as efficient as bare skin, but it is far better than the moisture-wicking materials I've used previously. Also, I've run in cotton in the same hot, dry environments with no issues at all.
- **Use cold water when available.** During a race, I take advantage of cold water (from aid stations or streams) and ice/snow by wrapping it in a bandana and placing it around my neck, dumping it over my head, or some variation of submerging myself. This will cool the body via conduction.
- **If all else fails, slow down.** Since movement generates heat, a lack of movement will cool the body quickly. I won't be so stubborn with stopping in the future.

In essence, we have to start treating thermoregulation as a separate variable that's not necessarily controlled by drinking more or popping more salt tabs.

Electrolytes

Back when I started running ultras, the consumption of supplemental electrolytes was more or less a given. If you were running long, you needed to be consuming a product like S! Caps, Salt Sticks, or good 'ole rock salt. The logic made sense- you had to replace the salt lost via sweat. When combined with water consumption, runners risked hyponatremia.

I would take one S! Cap about every hour or so depending on temperature. My sweat would get saltier and saltier, which led to burning eyes and chafing (salt deposits around the groin and armpits is much like having sex on a beach- grit + friction = unpleasant results).

Of course, the electrolytes DID dramatically reduce the danger of hyponatremia. The problem had more to do with an overconsumption of water, and the electrolyte overconsumption was an unfortunate side effect.

I had a lot of friends that read Tim Noaks' book "Waterlogged." I haven't read it myself, but their ad nauseum discussions pretty much summed up the plot: drink to thirst.

I started following this advice, first at the 2012 Grand Mesa 100 miler, then the 2012 TransRockies six day stage race, and lastly at the 2012 Grindstone 100 miler. In all three races, I cut my water consumption considerably... with no ill effects.

The other benefit- I didn't require any electrolyte supplementation. I did get some electrolytes from the various gels I ate, along with the half pound of bacon I ate ten hours before the race. Aside from that, I was electrolyte-free.

The result- my sweat was not especially salty. At Grindstone, I didn't have any salt-induced chafing issues. As long as I didn't over-drink, I had no need to supplement electrolytes.

But what about symptoms like cramping?

As I discussed in the section above, many in the ultrarunning community seem to believe hot temperatures can be remedied by drinking more water and taking more electrolytes. Unfortunately, the body only has a finite ability to cool itself via sweat (and moisture-wicking materials may dramatically reduce that ability). So... the solution isn't necessarily drinking more liquid and popping more salt. The solution could be taking steps to cool down. Here are a few:

- **Slow down.** Movement generates heat. More movement generates more heat. To cool down, slow down.
- **Seek shade.** No explanation needed.
- **Ditch clothes.** Unless the clothing is intended to reflect heat (white clothing in the desert) or act as a_solar furnace, less is more. If that means running naked, so be it. We're all beautiful... might as well show off your goods.
- **Get wet.** Dousing yourself with water facilitates evaporative cooling. Cooler water also helps cool the body (via conduction).
- **Expose yourself to a breeze.** This also helps facilitate evaporative cooling (via convection).

Reframing the problem from hydration/ electrolyte imbalance to thermoregulation has resulted in great success for me personally. I also have quite a few friends that have toyed around with these ideas and experienced similar positive results.

Chafing

Chafing is a significant problem in ultras. The longer you run, the more likely you are to chafe. Any place where anything comes in contact with skin, including other skin, is susceptible to chafing. Your long runs will give you ample opportunity to learn what areas chafe, how they chafe, and allow you to experiment with solutions.

Here are my suggestions for various areas:

- **Nipples:** Cover with adhesive bandages. I used to use duct tape, but the adhesive irritated the skin after long hours of exposure. For added protection, add a dab of your favorite sports lube to the nipple prior to applying the bandage.
- **Groin/thighs:** I've tried quite a few options- various lubes, tape, compression shorts, a kilt (added ventilation), and various states of trimming and/or shaving. I finally found short running shorts (current favorite = Brooks Infinity III) and a liberal dose of SportSlick brand lube work wonders.

130

- **Armpits:** The 'pits are difficult to protect. The only real option I found was good ole' lube.
- **Any area the clothing touches, including sports bras for the ladies:** Different articles of clothing will cause different levels of chafing. I prefer cotton shirts to technical shorts for this reason- the cotton is less abrasive. I usually treat trouble areas with a dab of lube or periodically change to a different style of clothing.
- **Hands (due to carrying water bottles):** My knuckles usually become chafed in long races. In cool weather, I've found fingered or fingerless gloves to be effective. In hot weather, I just lube up the knuckles.

The kilt kept the undercarriage chafe-free

132

Shave the Junk or Rock the 'Fro?

This is probably more of an issue for dudes, and wouldn't even be considered if it weren't for the "metrosexual movement" of the late 1990's and early 2000's.

Here's my "too much information" story. Around the time I started running ultras, I also started experimenting with various methods of trimming. It was done purely for aesthetics (Shelly liked it.) I was surprised to find two effects:

- Trimming kept the genitals cooler, and
- Trimming seemed to reduce chafing.

Seeing the positive effects of cutting back the schlong-fro, I decided to try shaving. As expected, the results were even better. Since that time, I've continued a routine of shaving.

A few tips and points to consider before giving your boys the Bruce Willis 'do:

1. When the hair starts to grow back, it's itchy as Hell for a few days. You have to either endure the discomfort or keep shaving at least once a week.

2. If trimming, don't use the closest setting on electric clippers. Loose skin can get caught between the blades. Yes, it hurts. A lot.

3. If shaving, it's much easier to trim first. Long hair is difficult to shave. I use the trimmer to shorten the hair, then bust out the razor.

4. Pleasure. Not to turn this into a sex manual or anything, but the skin-on-skin clitoral contact may be pleasurable for women.

Foot Care

The feet of a trail runner typically endure more punishment than road runners. The dynamic terrain, steep grades, dirt, gravel, sand, and water crossings can be brutal. Well-fitting shoes, good socks (if worn... you know how I feel about those damn cloth foot bags), and appropriate preventative measures can go a long way toward keeping your feet in good working condition.

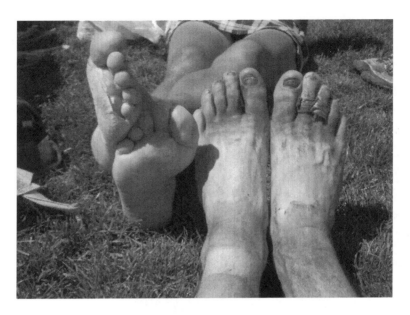

The biggest danger to your feet tends to be blisters. Knowing how blisters form is helpful to prevention. Jon VonHof's excellent book *"Fixing Your Feet"* discusses three variables needed for blisters to form: heat, moisture, and friction. In my experience, blisters can form with only one or two variables *if they are severe*. The key to prevention is managing all three.

To control moisture, start with a well-ventilated shoe. Ventilation allows sweat and water from water crossings or puddles to evaporate. Moisture-wicking socks also help keep the feet relatively dry. Some people like to use various powders on their feet, but I find they just turn to paste.

To control friction, start with shoes that fit the shape of your foot. Tie the shoes in a way that anchors the shoe to the foot to limit "sloppiness" of fit. If the shoes cannot be securely anchored, socks can be used to reduce friction. Some people even wear two thin pairs of socks. Lubrication can also be used. You should be able to determine where hot spots (friction points) occur during training runs. Lube those spots.

Heat is usually the most difficult variable to control. Ventilated shoes will help regulate foot temperature, but you're still at the mercy of the environment. Getting your feet wet is a common strategy, but it introduces the moisture variable. When training, purposely get your feet wet to test the draining and drying properties of your shoes and socks

Night Running

Running at night is a useful skill to develop. Many ultras have some degree of night running. Checking the start time and cutoff time of your race, then checking the morning and evening civil twilight times, is always a good idea. Civil twilight is the point where the sun is 6° below the horizon. In most cases, this is the time when it is possible to see your surroundings without a flashlight.

Running at night is relatively straight forward, just plan a few runs after dark. If I'm running a race that requires running through the night, I'll plan two types of runs: A very late run and a very early run. The late run usually starts around 10 p.m. and ends around 2 a.m. The early morning run starts around 2 a.m. and ends around 6 p.m. The idea is to acclimate your body to running during the hours you'd normally be sleeping.

If you will be using an artificial light, most people use either a handheld flashlight or a headlamp. I would recommend carrying both. Use the flashlight as the primary light source and the headlamp as a backup. Since the flashlight can be carried near the waist, it will cast longer shadows on the trail. This makes it easier identify and avoid obstacles like rocks, roots, and cobras. The headlamp is useful if you need hands-free light, like eating at aid stations or pooping.

Some ultrarunners strap a headlamp to their chest or waist. I've tried this method, but the light bounces too much. It also limits the ability to look to the side without having to move your entire body. Still, it may be a worthwhile experiment.

Sleep Deprivation Training

Doc Ott wrote a blog post about his strategy for ultra training:
http://www.docott.com/run/?m=201209

135

He came up with a method that allows him to hit high mileage and still spend time with his family.

His methodology brought back not-so-fond memories of my early days as an ultrarunner. I was more or less in the same boat- I had a finite amount of time to train but needed to build an endurance base to handle the rigors of ultramarathons. My solution was similar to his- wake up ridiculously early in the morning (2:00- 3:00 a.m.), run, get ready for work, drop kids off at daycare, work, pick kids up, engage in family time, put kids to bed, spend time with Shelly, go running again, sleep.

I did this for about a year. It served the purpose- I built a pretty good endurance base that has persisted for years. I also got a pretty decent string of sleep deprivation training runs since we had two babies that woke up throughout the night.

My experiences in 100 milers with this sleep deprivation training was mixed. I didn't get especially tired until after 4 a.m. I didn't get deliriously tired until sunrise, and the feeling persisted for about two hours. This wasn't a major issue until the 2011 Grindstone 100 when a 6 p.m. start coupled with a variety of other issues that led to a DNF.

I was determined to find a better method for overcoming sleep deprivation. The applicable science is pretty straight-forward. We normally have a 24 sleep-wake cycle which is one of many circadian cycles that regulate bodily processes. If we have a fairly predictable wake-up time, our body quickly adapts to specific periods of sleep and wakefulness. We have the ability to manipulate the sleep-wake cycle. If we stayed awake for 24 hours at a time, we'd eventually adapt to that sleep/wake cycle. Unfortunately we're continually confounded by the sun. We have light-sensitive photoreceptor cells in our eyes that "reset" our internal clock each day. Besides, those pesky "jobs" usually prevent unusual sleep/wake cycles.

The other biological issue is our biological need for sleep. We can't live without sleep. Literally. If we lose the ability to sleep, we die. A chemical called adenosine builds up in our bloodstream when we're awake. The longer we're awake, the more adenosine builds up. This chemical makes us feel sleepy, impairs cognitive function, and negatively affects coordination and balance, and a host of other undesirable effects that sabotage running.

136

Caffeine, the world's most popular psychoactive drug, works by temporarily blocking adenosine. One option in ultras is to drink a shit ton of caffeinated beverages. Indeed, Redbull and Monster are staples of my 100 miler drop bags. Unfortunately the effects are short-lived and result in a crashing effect after the adenosine-blocking wears off. You feel even more tired than you would if you hadn't consumed caffeine.

The other option is sleep, which dissipates adenosine. Interestingly, it doesn't take much sleep for this effect to occur. A 15 minute power nap should result in a significant reduction of adenosine. That's the biological basis for the "power nap." It's long enough to affect adenosine but short enough to prevent us from slipping into the deeper stages of sleep which makes us feel groggy upon waking. The problem-lying down and remaining immobile for 15 minutes at mile 70 almost always results in severe stiffness (not the morning wood type) and possibly exercise-induced cramping.

My Tested Solutions

I knew the two-a-day runs were not quite as effective as they needed to be based on Grindstone. I had a great opportunity to test a few different strategies at the 72 hour Across the Years race last December. I tried the 15 minute power nap, a 90 minute sleep period (to theoretically go through all five stages of sleep), and several variations of multiples of 90 minute sleep periods (three hours, four and-a-half hours, six hours).

I found four and a half worked well. Three was too short, as was 90 minutes. Unfortunately that didn't help much for hundos. There's no way I could give up three hours by sleeping. I'm not fast enough to create a large buffer for cutoff times. That essentially put me back to square one.

The Accidental Solution

Around late winter, Shelly and I decided to alter our travel methods. When we first hit the road and we had a long distance between clinics, we would break up the drive into 6-7 hour blocks. A drive halfway across the country might take us four days. Those travel days sucked because our kids were stir-crazy when we stopped. It took forever to calm them down. We decided to experiment with driving these routes in one block- through the night.

At first it was tough. I would stop several times for the aforementioned power nap. After three or four such trips, I noticed my "night endurance" increasing. I felt less drowsy. I had to stop less. I consumed less caffeine.

I didn't really consider the effects on hundos until Bighorn. The race was an 11 a.m. start, which guaranteed I'd be running through the night and well into the following day. Indeed, the race took me over 32 hours. Much to my surprise, I made it through the night with minimal sleep deprivation symptoms. I immediately made the driving connection.

The theory was sort of tested again at the Grand Mesa 100. Shelly and I ended up DNFing, but not before we got a healthy dose of night running. Again, I had very few sleep deprivation symptoms.

The final test was Grindstone. I woke up at 6 a.m. the morning of the race (kids are early risers and loud). The race didn't start until 6pm that evening. I didn't have any troubles that first night or the following day. I didn't run into any sleep deprivation symptoms until about 10 p.m. Saturday... 28 hours after the race started and 40 hours since I last slept. Even then, the symptoms were minor. I had trouble focusing on the trail, had some minor hallucinations, and felt a little drowsy. This represented a HUGE improvement from my experiences prior to Across the Years.

Conclusion

So... what would I recommend for sleep deprivation training?

Stay up all night occasionally. I do it about once monthly. Since it is tough physiologically, I don't recommend doing it more often.

I still question exactly why it was so effective. Did it cause my body to physiologically adapt to an occasional lack of sleep? Or am I simply learning to deal with the symptoms of sleep deprivation, thus reducing their severity? Or was it just a placebo effect and I just believe I can handle it better?

Learning When Shit's about to go Bad

This material is mostly redundant, but important enough to restate. This is the crux of ultrarunning- *learning to solve problems that arise.* When training in various bodily states, you get to experiment with quite a few different variables. Another significant advantage is learning to recognize the early signs of significant issues that plague ultrarunners. Here are some examples:

- **Glycogen or carbohydrate depletion:** As discussed earlier, your body has a finitely number of carbs to fuel your muscles. When the supply runs low, your body has to convert fat as a fuel source, which is a significantly slower process of delivering fuel to working muscles. This usually results in a crash or hitting "the wall", which is one of the most common causes of runners dropping out of a race (known as a DNF). Learning how this feels is among the most valuable skills you can learn. If you begin experiencing the early signs, consuming something sugary can prevent the crash.
- **Dehydration:** For me, recognizing the bodily sensations of early dehydration is difficult. Instead, I rely on other signs. I use urine frequency and color. If I'm peeing at least once every two hours and the urine color is clear or light yellow (like lemonade), I know I'm good. If I'm peeing less frequently or my urine is darker color (like apple juice), I know I'm nearing dehydration and will start drinking more. It's not an exact science, but still pretty effective. What about at night? I just shine a headlamp through the stream to determine color. Practice it a few times. What about women? [This answer comes from Shelly] She recommends learning to pee standing up (as opposed to squatting) and, like my suggestion, use a headlamp through the stream to determine color. Again, practice the technique. The technique also works well at truck stop bathrooms.
- **Sleep Deprivation:** Sleep deprivation is a major issue for me as evident by the previous sections, but usually only in longer races. If I'm excessively sleep deprived, my mood turns negative. I'm far more likely to stop a race due to sleep deprivation than anything else. The problem- sleep deprivation symptoms can be similar to glycogen depletion. Sleep deprivation is somewhat tricky because the best fix is actually sleeping. Loading up on stimulants may be a temporary fix (like pounding a Redbull or taking a few hits off the crack pipe). If that

solution doesn't work, it is possible to counteract some of the effects with a 15 minute "power nap."

- **Hyponatremia:** This is a life-threatening condition that is caused by too little sodium in your body. It usually results from consuming too much water and not enough sodium. Some symptoms are weight gain and swelling. The prevention is simple- take supplemental electrolytes during runs, especially if it is hot. I prefer Succeed S-Caps and will take one about every hour or two. Consuming sports drinks instead of straight water can also be useful, too.

Racing as Training

Running shorter races can be an excellent method of training for ultras. The races act as a quality training run and allow you to go through your pre-race routine. If the race is shorter, like a 5k, it will serve as good speedwork. If it is longer, like a half marathon, it will serve as a good long run.

Another great technique is to do a long run by running a race course prior to the race, then running the race afterward. I learned this technique from my friend Phil Stapert. He uses this idea to train for 100 milers.

This method can be especially useful if the race is run on the same course as your ultra. Check with the race director or the race website. They will usually be familiar with other races run on the same trails or roads

Coaching and Ultramarathons

Runners sometimes hire coaches, and the practice is increasing. Years ago, many people assumed running was simple enough to be done without guidance. Personally, I blame this idea for the horrible running form we often see at road races.

A running coach can teach you a litany of useful skills, including good running form. A running coach can also set up a training plan, monitor your progress, and recommend changes to improve your performance. Coaches can also provide necessary encouragement and moral support.

Running coaches are relatively easy to find online. Simply Google "running coach [your municipality]."

If you're looking for a specific ultra coach recommendation, the frequently-mentioned Jesse Scott is my top pick:_

http://jscott87.blogspot.com/.

If you're interested in coaching from me, I DO occasionally take on ultrarunning clients, though I usually prefer to coach running form on a short-term basis. Facebook is usually the best method to contact me:

http://facebook.com/robillardj

Does Body Type Matter?

Does ultrarunning require a rail-thin emaciated body type?

Not at all! If you look at the entire field in a typical ultra, you'll find runners representing every imaginable body type. Most of the elites, both male and female, tend to be on the thinner side. As soon as you get to the next-fastest group, all bets are off. All BMIs are represented.

Losing weight generally makes you more efficient, thus faster, but ultras are run at a slow enough speed to partially negate this effect. I'm not exactly thin myself. The last time I checked, by body fat percentage was somewhere around 15%. My "ideal" body weight is around 155 pounds. Currently I weigh around 185-190 pounds. In fact, I've gotten quite a few "If HE can run an ultra, I certainly can!" comments over the years. What can I say? I like food. And beer.

Don't let your body weight dissuade you from running an ultra!

Drop Bags

What is a drop bag?

A drop bag is some sort of container used to hold supplies needed during a race. The drop bag is dropped at some point along the race route. You will have access to the bag when you reach that part of the course.

Is a drop bag actually a Bag?

Not necessarily, though that is the most common container. Some people use backpacks, duffel bags, plastic shopping bags, or garbage bags. Other containers can be used, too. I like Rubbermaid containers. Some people use five gallon buckets. More or less any container will work, though it should be water-tight. Each race may have specific rules that dictate size, shape, and acceptable containers.

Do you NEED drop bags?

If you have a crew and that crew has access to every aid station where drop bags are allowed, then no. If your crew does not have access to some drop bag locations, they can be useful.

What goes IN the drop bags?

Drop bags can be used to stash almost any supplies needed for the race. Common contents include things like food, gels (technically food... but barely), electrolytes, first aid crap, lube, dry socks, spare clothes, rain gear, sun screen, insect repellent, anti-diarrhea meds, batteries, or whatever else you think you need. Maybe toss in a vibrator for a little "middle-of-the-race-natural-pain-relief" session?

How do you know if you pack too much?

For my first ultra, I had about 12 five-quart Rubbermaid containers full of assorted "goodies." Each drop "bag" was packed with everything I thought I would need. That turned out to be a huge mistake. When I arrived at the aid station, it took way too long to dig through the container to find what I needed. I had a ton of crap that just got in the way.

So how do you determine what is needed? Make a list of everything you think you need. Figure out what items will be available at the aid station and remove them from your list. Now eliminate unnecessary items (no need for batteries at an aid station you'll pass at noon.) Now put everything else in the drop bag. Go to an open field and throw it as far as you can. If you can't throw it more than 20 feet, you packed too much.

Pacers

A pacer is a runner that runs with you during an ultramarathon. In most cases, pacers are allowed to join you in the later stages of a race. While many shorter ultras allow pacers, they're most commonly found in 100 milers.

Pacers serve as a guide, motivator, coach, entertainer, and cheerleader. A pacer does so much more than simply set the running pace. A good pacer keeps you on the course. They remind you to eat and drink. They help you survive the lows and ride the highs. When the shit hits the fan and things go south, your pacer is there to problem-solve to get you to the finish line.

I've been fortunate to have a string of incredible pacers over the years. At the 2012 Grindstone100, Shelly paced me for the last 33 miles. While I didn't experience a serious low, there were a few times I was discouraged about the slow pace needed to climb the rocky mountain trails. She kept me distracted, reminded me to eat, and monitored my well-being. When we finally hit a runnable section, she encouraged me to run. When we hit the last 10 miles and I was fighting serious sleep deprivation, she took the lead on the trails to guide me through the rock fields.

I've had other great pacers, too. I credit my finish at Western States last year to Jeremiah Cataldo and Shelly. Jeremiah somehow managed to push me through 30+ miles in the darkness to put me in a position for a sub-24 hour finish, then Shelly closed the deal over the last eight miles.

Prior to that, I've been paced by Jesse Scott, Mark Robillard, Michael Helton, and Stuart Peterson... all did a fantastic job of leading me to my first two 100 miler finishes.

What Makes a Good Pacer?

It's tough to nail down exactly what qualities exemplify a great pacer because all runners will have slightly different needs. A good pacer should be able to adapt their strategies to maximize their runner's potential. Here are some considerations:

- **Pacing:** If the runner has a time goal, the pacer should try to set a pace that will reach said goal. The pacer should also be aware of contingency plans if that time goal is unattainable. Pushing too hard too early will usually result in a serious crash, which may lead the runner to drop from the race (DNF). The pacer has to be conservative, but not *too* conservative.
- **Position:** Does the runner prefer to lead or follow the pacer? Both positions have advantages and disadvantages. A pacer in the lead can look for course markings. A pacer that follows can closely monitor their runner. Since most predatory animals attack from behind, a dedicated pacer that chose to follow could really take one for the team. I usually prefer to lead unless I need to speed up or I'm crossing technical terrain and have trouble seeing the trail (like at night when really tired). Watching the pacer's foot placement makes it easier to navigate the technical stuff.
- **Problem-prevention:** A good pacer will recognize when the runner is about to have a problem. Did the runner suddenly get quiet? Maybe they're about to bonk (physical and psychological low caused by glycogen depletion). Did their running gait suddenly change? They may be developing a blister or other injury. Are they shivering or sweating profusely? They're too hot or too cold. Are they suddenly farting up a storm? They're having gastrointestinal distress. There are a thousand possible issues that can arise, and a good pacer will be able to recognize many of them *before* they become serious issues. I've been fortunate to have experienced ultrarunners (Shelly, Jeremiah, and Jesse) as pacers for the vast majority of my paced races. I regularly run with all three, so they know me well. They can predict problems a little earlier than someone that's not familiar with my idiosyncrasies.
- **Problem-solving:** Okay, so the pacer doesn't *always* catch problems before they become problems. If things DO go bad, the pacer is the runner's first line of defense to right the ship. This gets a little complicated because pacers can't "mule" (carry any gear for the runner), so the pacer can only work with whatever the runner is

carrying. The pacer may have to force the runner to eat, drink, speed up, sit down to rest, sleep briefly along the trail, hold their hair if they're puking, pop blisters, lube unsavory parts of their body... whatever. It's important for the pacer to know *how* to solve any problem that arises. This is why experienced ultrarunners usually make the best pacers. Alternatively, novice pacers should be well-read on the issues facing ultrarunners.

- **Develop thick skin.** I like to think I'm a fairly even-keeled ultrarunner... I try not to get too upset with my crew or pacers. However, running for 12+ hours tends to expose some raw nerves. A pacer should be ready for crabbiness and whining from their runner... and be ready to respond accordingly.
- **Knowing when to quit.** Most new ultrarunners take a "I'm going to finish no matter what" strategy, which works great in theory. In reality, it's unlikely most people have experienced the cornucopia of shittiness that can occur late in an ultra. I've met very few people that seem to have the ability to keep plugging along *no matter what* (Ryan Hansard and Katie Zopf, I'm talking about you). Everyone else will talk themselves into quitting at some point. A good pacer knows how to keep their runner going. They also know when it's best to throw in the towel and fight another day.
- **Experience or Familiarity?** My friend Vanessa asked if it's better to have a pacer that's an experienced ultrarunner that doesn't know you well or a newbie ultrarunner that does know you well. There are pros and cons to each. If you HAVE to choose, experience is probably a safer bet. If someone has run quite a few ultras, they will know a variety of solutions to common problems. Conversely, a newbie may know you well, but won't know how to fix unexpected problems that arise.

Learning to Become a Pacer

Learning to pace is pretty straight-forward. Do research and gain experience. The best places to gain research are ultra books like Bryon Powell's *"Relentless Forward Progress"* or Kevin Sayers' "Ultrunr" website. To gain experience, volunteer to work an aid station at the later stages of any ultramarathon. Volunteer to work as a crew member for someone running an ultra. Run an ultra yourself. Pay attention to other runners, pacers, and crew members. Be a sponge and absorb as much as you possibly can.

Crew

A crew is a person or group of people that help an ultramarathon runner complete the race by providing support along the course. The crew is sometimes known as "handlers", but I think the term is dorky. "Crew" sounds more like an entourage.

The crew will follow the runner from location to location. Most races have specific locations where a crew can meet their runner, which is almost always at specific aid stations. These aid stations are said to allow "crew access." Depending on the rules of the particular race, crew access is usually explicitly limited to the aid station itself. The crew can't help the runner along the course or even a few hundred meters before or after the aid station.

The experience of crewing is defined by long periods of waiting, followed by a minute or two of frantic activity, then driving to the next location and repeating the cycle.

The crew's responsibilities are somewhat similar to a pit crew in auto racing. Since the runner wants to waste as little time as possible at each stop, the crew must quickly identify and correct any problems. The crew must also keep the runner updated with information like their position relative to the cutoff times, place in the race (if the runner cares), any significant weather changes, or other pertinent information.

Crewing for Jesse Scott at Tahoe Rim, 2012

The crew also has to be self-sufficient. They have to be familiar with the course and race rules, know how to navigate from one crew access point to the next, and be prepared for the long hours of waiting. The crew should be prepared with their own food and water (eating from the aid stations is usually prohibited), chairs, something to keep them occupied, and clothing appropriate for the expected (and unexpected) weather conditions. For 100 milers, the crew should also be prepared to take turns sleeping through the night by having a somewhat comfortable resting place.

Crew Chief

I always like to appoint a crew chief that will be responsible for major decisions. This should be the person that is either the most experienced ultrarunner, most familiar with you as a runner, or the most level-headed. A combination of all three is ideal. The crew chief will delegate responsibilities to other crew members, assess the state of the runner, and make final decisions in the likely event the runner is too tired or fatigued to think clearly. The crew chief should also be the person to make a final decision about the runner dropping from a race.

Crew Meeting

Before the race, the runner and crew should discuss pertinent issues. The runner should have a plan in place for aid station strategies, what clothing options they'll have at each aid station, possible shoe changes, if they'll need a light at a particular place, and anything else that is relevant. The runner should also discuss the expected pace based on the race goals. The runner should also discuss contingency plans. For example, if the runner plans on a sub-24 hour pace, what happens if the runner experiences trouble? Do they have a backup goal? Will the runner be satisfied with a finish even if they're dead last and finish a few minutes before the cutoff?

It's also important to discuss situations that will result in the runner dropping from the race. Most runners dramatically underestimate the depth of the lows they will experience. *There will be a point where you will want to quit.* Discuss how the crew should handle this.

My preference is to keep going unless I have a serious injury that threatens life or limb. I'm usually happy with finishing ultras no matter how slow. I have a pretty hearty ego and don't mind finishing dead last. I've finished races after sustaining minor injuries that required 20-30 miles of walking. I also know most lows are temporary and instruct my crew to ignore my plea to drop if it only occurs at one or two aid stations. If I'm in a sustained low for more than a marathon, I'll usually drop.

When the crew meets the runner, they should have a checklist of things to do. I like my crews to do the following:

- **Make sure they (or a volunteer) refill my water bottles**
- **Remind me to get rid of any trash I may be carrying (remember, littering is a big no-no).**
- **Remind me to eat, tell me what foods the aid station has available.** This is important because aid stations don't always have all food choices readily available. Almost all use tables, but some stuff will spoil if exposed to warm temperatures for too long.
- **Ask me about chafing and remind me to lube up.** Nothing ruins a race faster than a chafed Johnson.
- **Ask me how my feet are doing; have new shoes and socks ready should I need to change.** I'll also have them help with untying if it's later in the race and I can't bend over.

- **Have a change of clothes ready and alert me of any weather changes in the immediate future.** If I'm wearing a spaghetti-strap tank top and there's an approaching snowstorm, they have to remind me to change.
- **Give me my flashlight and backup headlamp if it is close to dark, or take the lights if it's past sunrise.** If it's in the middle of the night, I may have them change batteries.
- **Have a chair ready if I need to sit down.** This can be dangerous; sitting tends to add significant time to aid station stops. However, some maintenance requires sitting (like feet.)
- **Cheer me up by making bad jokes.** Luckily my friends have a dark sense of humor that rivals my own. Off-color jokes play well at 4 a.m.
- **Provide boobs.** Shelly has been known to flash me during particularly low points. While it's not something all crews need to do, it's worth considering. Boobs can be a powerful motivator. "What about Shelly" you ask? She appreciates a good flash, too.

After the Race

Recovery from ultras takes some time. While our bodies are more than capable of phenomenal endurance feats, they do need recovery time. Exactly how much changes from one individual to the next, and also changes as a function of experience.

In my own early ultra experiences, a fifty miler would sideline me from running for at least a month. It would take several days before I could ascend or descent stairs, and maybe a week before I could walk with a relatively normal gait.

As my body adapted over the course of a few years, recovery time shrank. My last 100 miler (Grindstone) wasn't too bad. I was able to run slowly the very next day. I felt normal after about three days. I was able to get back to ultra distances within about ten days.

When first beginning, take recovery slow. Get to know how your body responds. You'll be much more susceptible to injury during the recovery period. Some in the shorter distance running community suggest taking two recovery days for each mile run. That's a little excessive for ultras. If you have no other guidelines, I would recommend two weeks with little or no running and a month before getting back to normal training as a decent baseline until you get to know how your body responds.

Some Additional Ultrarunning Tips

Running long distances can be difficult because you eventually hit a point where you will want to stop. If the distance is long enough, no amount of willpower or determination will get you to the finish line. However, there are a few tricks that can be used to help increase the odds.

Trick #1: Expect the pain. Ultras hurt. Acknowledging and expecting the pain is a good first step. It's also useful to know the pain is temporary. Most pains experienced during a race go away during the race. If not, they go away shortly after finishing. Before you start, write out a list of all the things that may hurt. The physical act of writing does something psychologically to make the experience more real. Forewarning leads to greater manageability.

Trick #2: Learn to discriminate between *"this is normal long-distance running pain"* **and** *"I'm hurt"* **pain**. This is difficult because it's usually learned with experience. In the moment, most forms of pain feel like you're doing permanent damage to your body. After a little experience, you begin to understand what different types of pain signal. For example, I know the soles of my feet are going to hurt really bad in an ultra. That's just one of the pains that goes away shortly after finishing, so I can ignore it during the race. At Bighorn this year, I had a sharp, shooting knee pain. It was unfamiliar and may have been a sign of injury. Instead of just "gutting it out", I changed my gait. Here's a more detailed description of learning pain discrimination:

http://barefootrunninguniversity.com/2012/06/13/when-running-hurts-discriminating-between-good-pain-and-bad-pain/

Trick #3: Learn to enjoy the pain. FAR too many ultrarunners use drugs to dull pain, which is flat-out stupid. The extreme physical exertion coupled with the negative effects of ibuprofen, acetaminophen, or even the opiates (Vicodin, codeine, etc.) is a recipe for disaster. If you need that shit, you're not ready to run the distances you're trying to run *or* you need a better pain coping mechanism.

Pain is a bodily process. All bodily processes are subject to classical conditioning. You know the people that develop weird fetishes? The process that was used to develop that fetish can be used to develop a "fetish" to pain. Yes, you can turn yourself into a certified masochist. The trick is to associate pain with something pleasurable.

What works best?

Sex.

Specifically, we want to associate pain with the flood of positive neurotransmitters released at orgasm. One method would be to repeatedly get a little action (or fly solo) on really long runs. Since there may be inherent danger (i.e., indecent exposure... we have a lot of prudish "seeing genitals will cause my head to explode" municipalities here in the U.S.), I'd recommend using a process called higher-order conditioning. We're essentially going to associate the pleasures of orgasm with a neutral stimulus so the neutral stimulus causes some of the same reaction. We'll then apply the neutral stimulus when we experience pain in long distance runs. Eventually the pain of the run itself will trigger the pleasurable response... and we begin to *enjoy* the pain. I give the dirty details here:

http://barefootrunninguniversity.com/2011/06/05/just-say-no-to-ibuprofen-and-some-pain-management-alternatives-including-an-adult-solution/

Trick #4: Manage the lows. People don't quit ultras when they're feeling good. They quit when they feel like shit. In long races, there are many things that will make you feel like shit. Pain is one. Hunger, cold, heat, dehydration, trashed muscles, chafing, blisters, sleep deprivation, darkness, malfunctioning equipment, gylcogen depletion, and loneliness are some other things that can contribute to lows. Knowing what causes each of these and how to correct them can help minimize their effect. The goal is to fix problems before they become too bad or compound with other problems. All of us can overcome one issue. Two...not a problem. It's when a lot of problems pile up that we run into problems. Each problem gives us a reason to quit, and the more reasons we compile the more we persuade ourselves we can't go on. This problem is amplified if we hit the lows going into an aid station where we can drop from the race.

This is basically what happened to Shelly and I at Grand Mesa in 2012. We were managing our lows nicely, then hit a situation where several new problems sprung up at the same time. The result? We decided to drop at about mile 60. Had we been better prepared, we probably could have salvaged the race.

Use training to practice this by purposely inducing specific lows. Run when tired, cold, and hungry, then try fixing the problems during the training run. By doing this repeatedly, you've be in a much better position to survive the lows during a race.

Trick #5: Shorten the race. Most beginning ultrarunners have a tendency to think of the number of miles remaining. If that number is big, it can seem insurmountable. At mile 55 of a hundo, thinking you still have 45 miles to go seriously blows, especially if you're in the middle of a low. Breaking the race down to shorter races from aid station to aid station can help. Psychologically, it's much easier running several three-to-eight mile races than 45 miles.

Again, use training runs as practice. Set up a loop, then run it repeatedly. I used to do this with a three mile loop that I'd run 10 times. In the middle of each loop, I'd only focus on finishing that loop. After a few such training runs, shortening the perception of the distances became easy.

Trick #6: Surround yourself with positive people. This includes your crew, your pacer(s), and other runners. You do not want to be around people that complain, point out the negative, or remind you that you're suffering. I've made the mistake of inviting negative people as crew members, and it didn't turn out well. Over the years, I've learned to be very selective of those I choose to be around in races (and life in general). I have about ten good friends I'd trust as crew members or pacers because I know their negative personality will never contribute to me failing. All of them like to have fun, dick around, and don't take anything too seriously. That's *exactly* what *I* need when I'm suffering.

Other runners on the course can be a problem, too. If I ever run with another runner and they start complaining, I either speed up or slow down. They have almost as much power to ruin a run as a bad crew or pacer.

It's fairly easy to figure out if someone isn't crewing material. If you use Facebook or other social media, lots of complaining posts are a red flag. Training runs can also be used. Take them on a difficult run. I'd suggest running on a hot day with limited water, or running in cold rain. If they complain a lot, you don't want them on your crew.

Trick #7: Surround yourself with people that know what they're doing *and* know you as a runner. My crew and pacers tend to be the runners I train with at least occasionally. I know they know me well enough to recognize when I'm having problems, what is causing the problems, and how to fix the problems. They're also experienced ultrarunners. They know what they're doing because they've been there themselves. This experience is absolutely invaluable. You're going to experience some bad things, especially in 100 milers. Having a calm crew that isn't going to freak out, can diagnose what's wrong, and take the appropriate action will keep you in a race. If I couldn't have at least one experienced crew member and/or pacer, I'd opt to go alone.

I see a lot of inexperienced crew members or pacers making really, really bad decisions. For example, a common mistake is to feed a runner salt if they're covered in dried salt. If the body is expelling excess salt, the last thing the runner needs is more. Experience is invaluable.

Trick #8: When things get bad, change something. Maybe change your shoes, socks, shirt, or ditch your water bottles for a hydration pack. Sometimes I even do something silly like brushing my teeth. The slight change in routine or stimuli can have a rejuvenation effect, which may help resurrect you from a low.

Trick #9: Speed up. While I discussed this earlier, it's worth mentioning again because it's so counter-intuitive. When we're in pain, fatigued, and feel like we've rolled down a very large, rocky hill, we tend to slow down. Walk even. Sometimes we'll feel better if we speed up. Change in gait activates muscles a little differently, helps stretch us out, and shaves a little time off our finishes.

There you have it- nine tips to help you get to the finish line of your next ultra. Most of them can be practiced in training, which will make them even more effective.

Random Life Tips

This material has little or nothing to do with ultras, but I have a tendency to over-share. If you're a stickler for staying on one topic, ignore this section. Otherwise, here are a few truly random "life tips" that will be part of a future book. Some are the result of my own experiences. Some are advice I received from others. A few even come from Internet memes. Enjoy!

- The best way to get anything, from love and affection to money and fame, is to not need it in the first place. The less you give a fuck, the easier life gets.
- We always think the next generation will be doomed because they haven't learned skills we deem to be essential. It's an illusion. In reality, they've been learning the skills they need to survive *their* word. Give them a break.
- If you ever get a flat tire, take a picture. In the future, you can use that picture for excuses.
- Communicate your needs. Expecting others to know what you need is a recipe for disappointment.
- If you're in a dangerous neighborhood and dress like a thug, you'll likely be safe. Criminals tend not to fuck with other criminals.
- It's almost always better to ask for forgiveness after trying something versus asking for permission before doing something. Most people say no as a result because they expect the worst.
- Avoid buying stuff on credit at all costs. Think of debt as a prison sentence that severely limits your freedom.
- Explosive diarrhea is a great excuse for anything. Nobody asks follow-up questions.
- The easiest way to accomplish anything usually involves finding the route nobody else is taking.
- Make a habit of picking up trash in public.
- Want to lose weight? Don't piss around with stupid diets or fad exercise equipment. Eat less and move more.
- Be willing to try anything once. You just might like it.
- Your imagination is the key to creative problem-solving, which is one of the keys to life success. Give yourself permission to daydream.
- Don't confuse what you *think* the world should be with what the world *is*.

- Vibrators can be used by dudes, too. The underside of the penis is almost as sensitive as the clitoris.
- When you start dating someone and they show up unexpectedly at work, deliver flowers, etc., it's usually not a romantic gesture. It's a form of pissing to mark their territory. That possessiveness is often a precursor to verbal or physical abuse.
- If you ever need advice and decide to use Internet forums, register with a female's name and use a picture of a hot woman as the avatar. You'll get answers A LOT faster.
- When you have to deliver criticism, use a positive sandwich. Give a sincere compliment, followed by the criticism, followed by another compliment.
- Both women and men are terrible at recognizing flirting behavior. Women often assume guys are just being nice when they're really flirting. Men often assume women are flirting when they're really just being nice. Women- assume all nice guys are really flirting. Guys- assume all flirty girls are really just being nice.
- Question everything. Start with your own beliefs, ideas, and principles.
- Don't try to make your life easy. Work to learn the skills that will allow you to navigate a difficult life (thanks for that tip, Bruce Lee.)
- Win or lose, sincerely thank your competition for making you better.
- You're never 100% ready for anything. Waiting until you feel ready is just an excuse to hide the fear of trying. Go for it. Which brings up...
- If you fear something, write down the worst-case scenario then come up with a plan should that happen. Once we actualize our fears, they become much easier to conquer.
- If you want to appear more attractive to a date or spice up a relationship with your significant other, do something exciting or mildly scary. The resulting rush is misinterpreted by our brains as attraction.
- Tip well. If you can't afford 15 to 25%, you shouldn't be eating out. If you can afford it and still leave shitty tips, you're a douche bag.
- As a parent, your job is to raise adults, not kids. Act accordingly.
- When you disagree with someone, spend your time looking for common ground instead of proving you're right.

About Us

I intentionally saved this topic for the end. I didn't want our story to dilute the rest of the information. This book, after all, is about YOUR journey, not mine. Quite honestly, I get annoyed when writers add a long "about me" section to a book (yes, I did that very thing in *The Barefoot Running Book*- I'm hypocritical that way.) I did want to add the section, though. Understanding the path my family has taken may help give some perspective to the topics in this book.

Shelly and I started our running obsession innocently enough- we wanted to lose a few pounds. We ran recreationally for about a year. She eventually convinced me to sign up for a local 15k road race, which gave me the racing bug. A friend of ours introduced me to the idea of ultramarathons. The concept sounded so stupid, I knew I had to try it.

Training for that ultramarathon led me to barefoot running. I always considered the two endeavors to be one in the same- barefoot running was a means to an end. It taught me how to run with better form which allowed me to run ultras. Running was a hobby for those first few years.

When Christopher McDougall published *Born to Run*, barefoot running took off. Since I already had a barefoot running blog (one of the few in existence at the time), I was thrust to the forefront of the barefoot running movement. My natural inclination to teach led to barefoot running clinics, which morphed into the barefoot book, which morphed into working with Merrell.

Eventually Shelly and I decided to leave our teaching jobs to chase our passions- travel and trail running. We spent close to two years on the road traveling throughout the United States, holding running clinics, running ultras, and exploring mountain trails.

Our home

After nearly two years of continuous travel, we decided we needed a break. We've since settled in the San Diego area. The temporary break has allowed me to reflect on our adventures and finally write this book.

We don't have definite plans for the future, but we've learned a valuable lesson thus far- live your life today and don't make dumb excuses. Life is too short to waste doing something you hate in the hopes of a brighter future. For many of you, this will mean embracing that spirit of adventure. Sign up for that race. Take that trail running vacation. Write that book even though you're completely unqualified. Follow your passions. *Start living today.*

Other Writing Projects

Like this book but want a greater diversity of topics? Check out some of my blogs!

- Barefoot Running University: The flagship blog covers barefoot and minimalist running, writing, lifestyle, and a host of other topics. http://barefootrunninguniversity.com

- Robillard Adventures: Our family's travels, more about our lifestyle. http://robillardadventures.com
- Squirrel Wipe: The blog that started this book project. http://squireelwipe.blogspot.com
- Sexpressionists: Sexuality and relationships. http://sexpressionists.blogspot.com
- Cupcake Fighting: Boxing, kickboxing, and Brazilian jiu jitsu. http://cupcakefighting.blogspot.com
- High School Survival: Education in general and teaching in particular. http://hs-survival.blogspot.com
- Death Coaches: Life coaching. Yes, you can hire Shelly and I to make your life better. http://deathcoaches.blogspot.com
- Shoeless Shelbell: Shelly's blog. http://shoelessshelbell.blogspot.com

Made in the USA
San Bernardino, CA
24 December 2018